About the author

Dr Arthur Dahl is a marine biologist educated at Stanford and the University of California, with primary research interests in coral reef ecology, marine algae and island environments. After several years as an associate curator at the Smithsonian Institution in Washington DC he moved to the South Pacific, where he served as the regional ecological adviser for the South Pacific Commission, 1974–82, and organized the South Pacific Regional Environment Programme. Subsequently, he worked as a consulting ecologist on a wide range of environmental and scientific topics for various governments and international organizations including IUCN, UNESCO and the Oceans and Coastal Areas Programme of the United Nations Environment Programme (UNEP).

Since 1989, Arthur Dahl has worked for UNEP full-time and is currently a deputy assistant executive director. In addition, he is coordinator of the UN's System-wide Earthwatch. He is responsible for developing international cooperation in monitoring the global environment, with a special interest in indicators of sustainable development.

He is the author of a large number of scientific publications in specialized journals, as well as *Unless and Until: A Bahá'í Focus on the Environment* (Bahá'í Publishing Trust, London, 1990).

The Eco Principle

Ecology and economics
in symbiosis

ARTHUR LYON DAHL

George Ronald
OXFORD

Zed Books Ltd
LONDON & NEW JERSEY

The views expressed herein are those of the author and do not necessarily reflect the views of the United Nations.

The Eco Principle: Ecology and economics in symbiosis was first published by Zed Books Ltd, 7 Cynthia Street, London N1 9JF, UK, and 165 First Avenue, Atlantic Highlands, New Jersey 07716, USA, and George Ronald, Publisher, 46 High Street, Kidlington, Oxfordshire OX5 2DN in 1996.

Cover designed by Andrew Corbett
Set in Monotype Garamond by Ewan Smith
Printed and bound in the United Kingdom
by Biddles Ltd, Guildford and King's Lynn

A catalogue record for this book is available from the British Library

US CIP data is available from the Library of Congress

Zed:
ISBN 1 85649 433 0 cased
ISBN 1 85649 434 9 limp

George Ronald:
ISBN 0 85398 412 3 limp

Contents

Foreword

We are driven in the modern world by news flashes, sound bites, short-term priorities and instant solutions. The pressing problems of the moment leave little time for reflection on their deeper causes and the broader perspectives for their solution.

It is thus always of particular interest when someone with extensive practical experience and an active involvement in the realities of this world stands back to view the larger picture, tries to ask fundamental questions and explores a range of possible answers. This book is such a work. It is particularly rare to find an approach that is so universal in its appeal and balanced in its coverage, with a message that is equally appropriate to industrialized and developing countries and to countries with economies in transition.

While each reader may bring a different viewpoint and may not share all the conclusions presented here, they cannot help but be challenged by this stimulating view of our economic, social and environmental situation. In a world where there is a general loss of any sense of direction, we need to rethink the underlying assumptions of our society, starting with a clear view of the essential values that must frame any new economic or social paradigm. Too many books today paint a gloomy picture of our future; here is one that tries to look constructively and optimistically at the exciting new potentials opening up before society as change accelerates around the world.

I commend this book to all concerned, thinking people, and hope that it will stimulate a lively and widespread dialogue on the transformations in all societies that are required to achieve a sustainable future.

Elizabeth Dowdeswell, Executive Director
United Nations Environment Programme

Author's preface

This book originated in my attempt to synthesize twenty-five years' experience dealing with issues of ecology, environment and economic development, as I launched into the challenging task of trying to define and apply the concept of sustainable development. To put these ideas in the context of other work in the field, it may help to summarize the path I have followed and thus my particular perspective.

As a budding biologist, I specialized in ecology (before it was a fashionable subject) because of my interest in biological systems and their relationships, starting with the mechanisms of simple marine algae at the cellular and sub-cellular levels, and gradually expanding to plant-environment interactions and the structure and function of complex ecosystems like coral reefs. The beginning of my professional career in scientific research caught the crest of the first wave of environmental interest in the late 1960s and early 1970s, when the Club of Rome was debating the 'Limits to Growth', Schumacher published *Small is Beautiful*, appropriate technology and ecodevelopment were widely discussed, and the United Nations held the Stockholm Conference on the Human Environment (1972) and launched the United Nations Environment Programme. I participated at Stockholm as an observer for the Bahá'í International Community in both the governmental conference and the non-governmental organization forum. As a life-long Bahá'í, I have always been interested in what leads to harmony and unity in systems, including social systems and value systems, and their relationships to the other kinds of systems operating on this planet. This has inevitably coloured my whole approach to science and to the synthesis of many fields in this volume.

A long-standing concern for the problems of developing countries led me in 1974 to leave my career in basic ecological research on coral reefs to become regional ecological adviser to twenty-two small island countries and territories of the South Pacific. I moved to New Caledonia and laid the foundations for the South Pacific Regional Environment Programme. For two decades I lived and worked mostly in developing countries, assisting governments and international organizations with the practical problems of environment and development, often at, or close to, the grass roots. I was thus largely cut off from the intellectual and academic debates of the past twenty years, except for what could be gleaned from the magazines and newspapers to which I had occasional access. Apart from a couple of undergraduate courses in economics thirty years ago, my experience in economics and social sciences comes only from dealing with practical problems in the field. My approach to these fields is thus more intuitive than scholarly, and my knowledge of their professional literature is far less than might be desirable. However, experience with the practical realities faced by many countries and communities can be more valid for the type of analysis presented here than abstract academic training.

I joined the United Nations Environment Programme in 1989, first with the Oceans and Coastal Areas programme, building regional cooperation among countries sharing a common coastal and marine environment. I spent some months in the Secretariat of the United Nations Conference on Environment and Development (the Rio Earth Summit of 1992) to work on the drafting of its Agenda 21, which encouraged my broader reflections on the meaning of sustainability. My next responsibility was coordinating the United Nations (UN) system-wide Earthwatch, including helping the UN to define indicators for sustainable development. It was my personal preparation for this task that led to this book.

This book thus distils insights based on experience ranging from remote tribal villages to global negotiating forums. In addressing the roots of the problems in today's society, I attempted to synthesize and draw conclusions from my scientific background in ecology and the nature of complex systems, combined with practical experience in many developing countries, and a value system founded in my Bahá'í beliefs. It was only when the first version of the manuscript was circulated to some publishers and friends for review that my attention was drawn to the extensive and stimulating work by others on many of the issues raised, with which my own thoughts had independently or unconsciously converged. The wide range of subjects touched on have made it impossible, in the midst of a busy professional life, to search out and refer to all the relevant literature. I have tried, in preparing the manuscript for publication, to emphasize those ideas that complement or extend current thinking, and to provide some cross-references to pertinent works which I have been able to locate and skim. Unfortunately, my time for this was limited as I was working full-time on trying to implement those aspects of the action plan adopted at the Earth Summit in Rio for which I am responsible.

This book can thus not pretend to be a thorough academic study, but is only an attempt by a practitioner to contribute a particular perspective to the debate on our future. I must acknowledge with appreciation those, including Lawrence Arturo, John Beckett, Gregory Dahl, Carl Djerassi, John Huddleston, Dorothy Marcic, Alfred Neumann and George Starcher, who have found my approach sufficiently interesting to provide comments and to encourage me to pursue its publication. I should also apologize to all those who have probably gone much further than I have in many of the fields considered but whose work has escaped my notice and not been cited, or not been treated with the depth it deserves.

I hope that the ideas presented here will stimulate further reflection and research by those more qualified than I am in these fields. In particular, I hope that the economists who read this book will begin to see their work in a wider social and ecological context, that environmentalist readers find ways to integrate their work with the social sciences, and that both come to see the pertinence of human values to their efforts.

Arthur Lyon Dahl

CHAPTER I

Paradigms in conflict

Economy and ecology, words for two of the fundamental concepts of modern society, share the same Greek root, *oikos*, meaning 'house' or 'habitat'. Economy refers to how to manage our house, and ecology how to know or understand it. This unity of word roots also reflects an underlying unity of purpose and function that should link ecology and economy. However, in practice, each discipline lives largely in a separate world, speaking a different language, applying different principles, starting from very different underlying assumptions, and reflecting often conflicting paradigms. The chasm between economics and ecology is a symptom of the malfunctioning of modern society which threatens our very future. Each discipline is grappling with difficult and apparently unmanageable problems within its own framework.

On the economic side, the repeated cycles of boom and recession, the instabilities in international economic relations, and the resulting crises that have shaken nations and whole regions, show our imperfect understanding and management of economic systems. The growing divide between the wealthy industrialized and poor developing countries demonstrates how unbalanced and unstable the present world economy is, and that instability carries considerable risks for the immediate future. While individual elements of economic theory and practice have shown their value, the problem is with the whole rather than the parts. There are fundamental gaps and inconsistencies in modern economic planning and management that are at the root of some of our most serious problems, such as poverty, unemployment, the debt crisis and the growing gap between the richest and poorest nations.

Ecology raises another set of issues through the environment movement and the scientific work exposing such problems as the health effects of pollution, damage to the ozone layer, and the greenhouse effect which threatens to cause global warming. Human activities have finally reached a scale where they are having an impact on the whole planet. For the first time, we are running into limits from which we cannot escape just by moving on to some new frontier. In the past we were able to neglect the way we used and discarded many things because they simply vanished into nature, dwarfed by the size of natural systems and absorbed into them. Today, humans are the dominant species on this planet and we have unwittingly taken on the responsibility for its management. However, we are still far from having either the knowledge or the wisdom to do so effectively.

These two sets of issues were drawn together and publicized by the United Nations-sponsored World Commission on Environment and Development (the Brundtland Commission) in their report *Our Common Future*, which developed the concept of sustainable development integrating environment (ecology) and development (economy) in the broad context of global society. The Commission defined sustainable development as development that meets the needs of the present generation without sacrificing the ability of future generations to meet their own needs. At the Rio 'Earth Summit' (the United Nations Conference on Environment and Development – UNCED) in 1992, governments represented by over one hundred heads of state and government adopted sustainable development as a central theme for action into the twenty-first century, as embodied in the global action plan, Agenda 21. Agenda 21 makes many specific recommendations in almost every field related to environment and development. However, it did not succeed in addressing the root causes of these problems, because they are not well understood and because the political issues they raise are too sensitive for most politicians to be able to face them directly. For instance, there is no consensus on what development really is or should be, since the example of development in the industrialized countries is, in many ways, unsustainable. Everyone agrees that poverty is undesirable, but there are few clear ideas as to how to eliminate it or what a poverty-free society should be like. The challenge now is to form a working concept of sustainable development, and to find how, in a practical way, it can be implemented, both collectively in society and individually by each person.

Sustainable development requires the integration of economics and ecology. Yet how is this possible when the two fields are so fundamentally different? Most economics practitioners are not prepared to stand back and question the frameworks, assumptions and beliefs on which their careers and whole lives have been built. Market economics is now as much of an established dogma as Catholicism was at the time of the Christian Reformation in Europe, when the early Protestants challenged the established Church. This book is an attempt to bridge the gap between ecology and economics. For economists and those attached to the Western free-market model of development, it proposes a larger framework within which economics needs to evolve and adapt. For ecologists and environmentalists, it tries to link economic realities with the scientific framework of ecology and the approaches of systems analysis. For those rooted in one of the religious traditions, which have been increasingly marginalized in Western thinking, it aims to integrate the spiritual dimension into both economics and ecology.

The world is searching for direction, for models and ideals, that will help it to chart a course towards a better future, when so many trends are in the wrong direction. The two great ideologies of capitalism and socialism have failed to deliver their promised results.[1] The communist system of the former Soviet Union has collapsed and other socialist states and parties are searching for new ideological and economic bearings. The market system is proposed as a universal panacea, yet it is aggravating the plight of starving millions while allowing a small minority to live in undreamed of affluence. People in all walks of life, with all kinds of responsibilities, whether in government or religion, in business or academia, in industrialized or developing countries, are bewildered by the pace of change as we are swept along towards an uncertain and in many ways threatening future. We lack answers and do not know how to respond or in what direction to try to move society.

This book attempts to stimulate reflection and debate on these fundamental issues. It proposes a framework to unite economics, ecology and some of the significant social dimensions of our world as we move towards a global society. It addresses both the role of governments, businesses and other social institutions, and the attitudes, values and behaviour of each individual as he or she can contribute to social change. It takes as its underlying assumption that science, technology, communications, transport and commerce have united the world physically, steadily increasing our levels of interdependence and mutual awareness.

The problems that we face today are in many ways the symptoms of the effort of human society to come to terms with this fundamental change in our physical and social environment. Some of the most violent and tragic responses have been reactionary, resisting the forces for change and integration, and tearing nations and peoples apart in the process. Whether originating in ethnic violence founded in deeply rooted prejudices, in religious conflict and fundamentalism, in petty power struggles between factional leaders and warlords, in the random explosions of the dispossessed and marginalized with no hope for the future, or in some combination of these forces, a new wave of insecurity, chronic violence, bloodshed and suffering is sweeping the world. Other responses to the physical unification of the world are more constructive, but they still struggle against the enormous inertia in our societies.

The fundamental approach in this book is that of a broad-brush overview of the challenge our civilization faces, with just enough of a theoretical framework to illustrate the problems and processes under consideration, without going into the detail and documentation required of a scholarly treatise. The necessary breadth of viewpoint required to treat the subject for the general reader has meant that depth has had to be sacrificed. While it might have been interesting to explore the evolution of Western thinking as it relates to the economic and environmental problems we face, there has been no attempt here at historical analysis. Detailed studies can always come later, prepared by suitable experts in each field, within this general framework. The aim is to cut through the cluttering detail of our human complexity and social diversity in a search for underlying principles that can help us to redefine our relationships to each other and to the world around us. Of course, it is not possible to provide all the answers; the challenge now is to learn to ask the right questions. If this book stimulates the reader to question his or her fundamental assumptions about the world as we know it, it will have accomplished its purpose.

The ideas and approaches raised here will be rejected in some quarters, since they threaten many of the foundations and assumptions on which Western society, and many successful careers, have been built. Yet even those who may disagree with the alternatives proposed need to ask what else they will put in place to address the fundamental failures in our present system.

This book was written from the perspective of an ecologist, applying the scientific techniques and approaches used to study the operation of natural systems to analyse the whole human ecosystem. It identifies the dimensions and controlling factors that define our environment, including the modern social expressions of the human organism. In this sense the approach is basically scientific and reflects what is in many ways a viewpoint rooted in a Western intellectual framework. For those from other cultural and intellectual traditions where, for instance, the individual is not the centre of reality and progress is an unfamiliar concept, the line of thought developed here may reflect unconscious biases, but this can probably not be avoided in any single-authored work.

This work also draws inspiration, and many essential concepts too numerous to cite individually, from the writings of Bahá'u'lláh and the Bahá'í Faith,[2] which define the underlying values and structures necessary for a future world society. It is the creative interaction of Bahá'u'lláh's profound vision of human nature and purpose, and of the scientific method as developed in the science of ecology, that stimulated the thinking behind the chapters that follow. Hopefully, this combination of the scientific and the spiritual, of Western and Eastern thought, will assist in the challenging task of integrating the natural world and human society necessary to achieve sustainable development.

The need for the integration of economics and ecology has been widely evident, and many other thinkers are also working on aspects of the ideas and principles discussed here. It has not been possible to document all the pertinent literature across the wide range of fields touched on, although some references to key works accessible to the author have been provided where possible. The convergence of these lines of thought from various sources and fields itself illustrates the timeliness of this approach.

The plan of the book follows a logical sequence. Chapters 2 and 3 describe the critical problems of present society, first from an economic and then from a more environmental perspective. Neither will have much that is new for those already specialized in one or the other field, and their view of present society can be depressing, but they lay the foundations for the more positive and constructive chapters that follow. Consider them the darkness before the dawn. Chapter 4 introduces the key definitions and theoretical concepts of the theory of 'ecos', which is developed here as a tool to analyse the complex problems of today and to identify where to look for solutions. This theory introduces the idea of functional units, for which I have coined the term 'ecos', and their essential characteristics as they apply to both ecological and economic entities. It will assist in understanding the subsequent chapters in their broader context. However, if it seems too abstract, skim it (the key points are in italic) and go on to the more concrete chapters that follow. It can always be re-read later once the theory has been related to specific subjects of interest. Chapters 5 to 8 apply this analytical approach of ecos to the natural world, economics, humans as individuals and in communities and institutions, in a search for insights as to new and better ways to address and solve the problems that seem today to overwhelm us. Chapter 9 summarizes the essential points and concludes with a vision of the future society that could evolve if we are willing to make the effort to change.

It should be obvious from the above outline that this is a book that should be read from front to back, rather than dipped into. Like a hike in the mountains, an effort is required along the way, but hopefully the vistas from the top will provide an ample reward.

Notes

(For full references see selected bibliography)

1. For a more complete analysis of future directions as they relate to the need for world peace, see Universal House of Justice (1985) *The Promise of World Peace*.

2. Among the many works of Bahá'u'lláh, sources for this book have included *Gleanings from the Writings of Bahá'u'lláh*, *The Hidden Words of Bahá'u'lláh*, and the *Kitáb-i-Aqdas*, Bahá'u'lláh's book of laws. Other pertinent Bahá'í references include 'Abdu'l-Bahá, *Foundations of World Unity* and *The Secret of Divine Civilization*, and Shoghi Effendi, *The World Order of Bahá'u'lláh*.

CHAPTER 2

It isn't working

Western civilization has reached heights of material development exceeding all past expectations, and there is a frequent tendency in movies, science fiction and futurist projections to assume that progress will continue in the same direction. A dip in the economic growth rate of the industrialized countries is a major crisis. It is said that when America sneezes, the rest of the world catches cold. The rest of the world aspires to the same standard of living enjoyed in Europe, North America, Japan and a few other countries. Capitalism is triumphant and the consumer economy is the model governments around the world are trying to follow. Yet history documents many civilizations whose very success bore the seeds of their own destruction. What makes us think that we can avoid such a fate, when many of the signs are the same? Any proper diagnosis has to be based on a careful analysis of the symptoms.

The following critique of the present world social and economic system highlights a few of the areas where pride in our accomplishments may have blinded us to larger truths. It raises questions which will find some solutions, or at least sign posts to the new directions to take, in the chapters that follow.

Economics trapped in its own specialization

Ever since the Renaissance men of the sixteenth century, who seemed to be able to do many things well (Leonardo da Vinci was a good example), there has been a tendency in our society towards increasing specialization. Anyone today who tries to excel in several fields is looked down upon as a dilettante. Specialization is necessary and logical because the explosion of knowledge has made it harder and harder to keep up, so that each individual is driven to know more about less, as fields become increasingly narrow. The natural desire for mastery in a discipline has also led to various mechanisms to maintain exclusiveness, such as arcane vocabularies and a refusal to accept that 'non-specialists' can have anything to contribute to a technical debate.

While the result has been enormous progress across many fields of human endeavour, it also has increased our tendency to lose sight of the broader picture. Each speciality works to achieve a structure that is satisfying and internally consistent, without realizing or being willing to admit that its greatest weakness may be in its underlying assumptions or in areas outside its immediate scope or application. A change in assumptions can produce a complete transformation. For instance, the science of geology was revolutionized in the 1960s by the resurrection and acceptance of the concept of continental drift, based on the newly discovered mechanisms of plate tectonics. This change in the underlying assumptions of geology, from that of a static crust to one of shifting and colliding plates, radically altered scientific understanding of the mechanisms by which the geological record was built up.

The science of economics today seems equally vulnerable. Its foundations lie in the application of the mechanistic and reductionistic approaches of nineteenth-century science to human productive behaviour,[1] with concepts such as utility and production borrowed from analytical mechanics. The world has changed, even within science, but these assumptions have seldom been questioned. The various schools of economics have been created and refined to explain the workings of our economy and to guide efforts to manage it. Each specialty seems consistent and seems to have proven itself in the successes of the capitalist world in the post-war period, although recent experience has been less than ideal.

The collapse, like a house of cards, of the communist economy and political structure of the Soviet Union, was seen as the triumph of the Western market economies. Yet that collapse came largely from within, not without. There were fundamental flaws in the underlying assumptions of the Marxist-Leninist system as it was applied in the USSR, with resulting imbalances that led ultimately to an economic and political dead end, despite apparent success along the way. This example should be adequate warning for those within the Western capitalist free-market system, and those trying to emulate it, to look more closely at its own underlying assumptions. No matter how elaborate and well-built a structure may be, if its foundations are sand, its future is shaky.

Economics as if people didn't matter

The capitalist system may seem to make sense and to respond to the requirements of the dominant Western economies, suffering only temporary flaws and aberrations, yet it may equally have fundamental weaknesses that are not apparent because they are beyond the view of the different economic specialties. We have lost the perspective of the whole and are quite satisfied with our bits and pieces. Economics is only one dimension of the complex system that maintains human life and civilization on this planet. Since the socio-economic dimension preoccupies us at present, it may help to look at some of its flaws, before standing back to try to see the whole in a broader perspective.

The great weakness of economics as it is applied today is that it deals with only that part of the human system that is traded or marketed. Even within the field of the production of goods and services, it only covers those productive activities within the cash economy. Many activities which could be considered productive employment are ignored simply because they are not paid for or traded, such as subsistence agriculture and fisheries in many developing countries, or the work of women as housewives and in providing basic family needs (a housewife does not earn a salary). This undervalues, in particular, much of the contribution of women and the productive activities of most of the world's poor. It is, in practice, the economics of the rich.

Money is the language of economics. Just as words symbolize a physical or intellectual reality, so money today symbolizes the value we attach to things. When given as a salary, it represents the value of the work performed; when exchanged for an object or commodity, it represents the value or price we attach to the commodity. The fact that it can be represented by a bit of fancily printed paper, some numbers on a cheque, or a few magnetic squiggles in a bank's computer, shows how symbolic it really is.

Economists like to measure everything in monetary terms. If you can buy it or sell it, it has a value, and is thus within the scope of economics. This leads to measures like productivity, capital investment, value added, depreciation, and to the broader indices of success in the modern ranking of nations such as Gross National Product (GNP – a standard measure of economic activity), Gross Domestic Product (GDP) or per capita income. The problem is that many things cannot be measured in monetary terms, like human satisfaction, literacy, natural beauty, equality, safe neighbourhoods, or the privilege of breathing clean air. Since economics cannot easily be applied to such things, they are treated as externalities, which means that they are ignored by traditional economic systems of accounts.

The problem today is that most leaders place economics at the centre of our societies, often to the exclusion of other values, which are left to some subjective appreciation at the political or cultural level, if at all. Thus, material values that can be measured in money are given great importance and are used to demonstrate the success of nations and to define development. Other factors which might be equally if not more important to the quality of human life are generally ignored.

For many people in the West, money has gone beyond being a simple instrument to facilitate exchanges, or a symbolic language for calculating relative values, to become *the* central value, love and preoccupation in their lives.[2] It is no longer a means, but an end in itself. A man's worth is measured by his fortune, and modern status symbols are designed to show how much he can afford to spend. The worth of paintings is determined by how much they sell for at auction. There are even attempts to buy with money the immortality that the biological body cannot provide. Everything is reduced to its monetary value; other values are subordinated to, and sacrificed for, money. Profit has become the all-important measure of success, and not simply a sign of fiscal efficiency.

The present economic definitions of development lead to some surprisingly illogical results. Take, for instance, the standard measure of GNP, which was originally developed by the Americans during World War II to measure their success in the production of war goods, and which is now used to determine the size of a nation's economy. If a factory produces air pollution, the damage caused to human health, or to forests from acid rain, is not counted as a cost because the factory owner does not have to pay, as the damage may be distant and not easy to value or to trace to a particular source. However, the increased work for doctors, hospitals and pharma-ceutical companies to treat the illnesses caused by the pollution counts as economic activity and therefore as development and in-creases the GNP. The installation of pollution control equipment would also count as development. The substitution of a cleaner technology would also count initially as development, but the reduc-tion in economic activity from less pollution control and fewer sick people to treat would show negatively in the accounts. Gross National Product measures economic activity regardless of whether it is constructive or destructive, making it a poor measure of development. Armaments manufacture does wonders for GNP (as long as the war is fought somewhere else) even though most of what is produced is destined for immediate destruction. Only now are some significant attempts being made to reflect the negative side of development more realistically, and to incorporate environmental factors into net measures or satellite accounts, as in the UNDP Human Development Reports[3] and the new System of National Accounts adopted by the United Nations in 1993.

The market

According to economists, a market-based economy, in which everyone has the freedom to buy and sell, and prices can find their own level based on supply and demand, is basically an efficient mechanism, at least for items which have a monetary value and are traded. Problems are attributed not to the abstract principle but to its application. The powerful are tempted to manipulate a situation for their greater profit. Even the most committed free-market nations have had to prevent monopolies from developing, to control cartels and price-fixing, and otherwise to encourage competition and the play of market forces. Weaker governments may not be able to stand up to the pressures and temptations of those with economic wealth and power. The difficulty is that economists apply their model everywhere without understanding if it is appropriate.

The concept of the free market assumes complete knowledge of the supply and the demand. If the buyer knows there is a surplus, he or she will bid down the price or shop around. If a producer knows that market saturation will bring the price below the cost of production, he or she will produce less. In practice, however, poor or misleading information often leads to inefficiencies or manipulation. Since market knowledge is worth money, it is often concealed or controlled. Time lags in production processes can make it hard to adjust to rapid fluctuations, such as in agriculture where an annual planting cycle allows only for annual adjustments, a delay that can extend for tree crops to five to ten years or more. Bad communications can hinder access to market information, particularly for the poor, the uneducated, the remote and those in developing countries.

The normal operation of the market with the desire of each seller for an increased market share has pushed the consumer society far beyond any pure rationality. Advertising may serve not only to inform, but also to create an artificial demand for something which may in some cases be useless or even harmful, or to favour one product over a competitor's for no objective reason. Competing brands may be senselessly multiplied, sometimes even from the same company, with no significant difference in the product. Practices such as planned obsolescence, the use of sex symbols in advertising, cultivating a prestige or luxury image, and elaborate packaging, all play on emotion rather than on rational consumer choice. Enormous promotional budgets go into such manipulations and are passed on to the consumers. Buying becomes an emotional or almost pathological experience in such a consumer culture. All these practices mean that some buyers pay more, or sellers get less, than they would in a perfect market, and the distortions almost always benefit the already rich and powerful. The ultimate conclusion is that there is no perfect market; we do not know how to make a market mechanism operate justly and efficiently in our present society. The principal defenders of the free market today are generally those who stand to benefit the most from its distortions, or who have built an academic career from analysing and describing it.

Other problems come from the fact that markets exist at many geographic scales from local and national to regional and global. While expanding the size of the market should increase its efficiency (as in the case of the European Common Market or the North American Free Trade Agreement), increased size also aggravates the problems of the free flow of information mentioned above. Large size favours those who can afford the most elaborate and extensive information networks. In addition, the institutions that have been created to regulate global or regional markets are still weak, and many nations and regional groupings put their own benefit above the free functioning of the market by erecting protectionist barriers to trade or dumping subsidized products abroad. While multinational corporations have expanded to the global scale and thus escaped from national jurisdictions, there is presently no real global protection against monopoly practices or cartels, just as there are few global mechanisms for most other aspects of economic management.

As a result, the prices of primary commodities produced by developing countries continue to decline, while the prices of many manufactured goods have risen, resulting in increasingly unfavourable terms of trade and the inability of many countries to service their debts. The poor tropical countries try desperately to sell their produce and minerals, so that they can earn foreign currency to repay loans and buy essential imports. Tropical primary products like coffee, cocoa, and palm and coconut oil are tree crops with long lead times from planting to first harvest. Farmers and investors plant when prices are high, often for temporary reasons, but by the time the trees start bearing, prices are often driven lower by the increased supply. Mines also require lengthy prospecting and development and high initial investment, obliging producers to sell their output regardless of price if only to reduce their losses. International buyers can easily force prices lower in these conditions. Even in manufactured goods, the advantage goes to those at the technological cutting edge, where new markets are created and the seller can set prices. For more established technologies, it is still possible to compete when productivity increases lower the cost. However, as technologies like steel-making mature and more countries try to industrialize and develop import substitution, the competitive advantage of newness disappears, and such industrial production shifts to those countries that keep their costs down with low wages, poor social welfare provisions and little environmental regulation. While these shifts do bring some wealth to poorer countries and are often sought by their leaders, they also exploit the economic and social weakness of those countries and their people. In the face of this competition, wealthy countries with high labour costs and environmental standards must either abandon such industries or shield them behind protectionist barriers.

One of the fundamental problems with the move to free international markets is the extreme differences in currency values, wage levels and standards of living in different countries, aggravated by long-standing protectionist measures, often in the name of national independence and security. Since capital can now flow freely between countries but labour cannot, the removal of such protection favours investments in and exports from poor countries with low wages and little social security or environmental protection, which can produce things cheaply, even if at a high human and environmental cost. Wealthy nations must either reduce their costly standard of living in order to compete, or close down whole sectors of industry and agriculture which have been made uncompetitive, with all of the economic, social and political problems that follow. Thus, even where change is desirable and is recognized as needed, the adjustment may bring with it economic and social costs in both exporting and importing countries that must be considered.

Open international markets also allow multinational corporations to sell not only their products, but also the values of materialism and consumerism on which they flourish, frequently undermining local cultures and value systems already weakened by the rapid changes in world societies.

Waste and war as economic forces

One of the more frightening dimensions of the economies of the Western industrialized countries is the extent to which they are dependent for a significant part of their economic activity on production that is not aimed at essential human needs or real social benefits, such as luxury goods and fashions, alcohol and tobacco, which are driven more by tastes artificially cultivated for commercial benefit. Even worse is the major share occupied by military preparations and armaments development and manufacture. Investment in military goods and facilities does not build productive national wealth. On the contrary, they are designed to destroy and be destroyed. They require enormous research establishments of highly qualified scientists and engineers to design, and elaborate industrial facilities to manufacture. Once this military-industrial complex has been created, it acquires an inertia of its own, with thousands of careers and the well-being of whole communities dependent on it. Sudden peace would be such an economic and social disaster as to be unthinkable, although everyone pays lip service to the ideal of peace.

A corollary of this problem is the contradiction (one might even say hypocrisy) it produces in international affairs, where political leaders alternate initiatives to bring peace to some strife-torn region, and missions to friendly countries to sign major arms deals. There is the occasional embarrassment when a formerly 'friendly' country turns around and uses those same arms against those who made and sold them, but these are quickly forgotten. There seem to be morally water-tight compartments in those countries, which defend the economic benefit of arms factories and see every new arms sale as a victory over the competition, while expressing indignation and horror when the products of these activities are used to slaughter women and children and to destroy generations of effort in development.

When viewed in the context of the global imbalance between

rich and poor and the death and suffering of the starving millions, the wastage of intellectual and material wealth in warfare, both through the production of arms and the employment of millions in the military services, and in the use of these resources in the destruction of so many lives, not to mention laying waste to cities, industries and agricultural areas, setting countries back decades in their development efforts, stands out as perhaps the most obscene absurdity of our modern so-called 'civilization'.

One simple illustration of the tragedy and stupidity of warfare is the widespread use of antipersonnel mines. These simple and dia- bolical devices are mass-produced in industrialized countries, like plastic toys, at a cost of a dollar or two, which is well within the reach of even the poorest army or rebel group. They are easily scattered by land or air, and can be almost impossible to detect until an innocent child steps on one and loses a leg or two. Tens of millions have been spread across all the sites of conflict, and they continue to kill and maim long after the fighting has ended, making major areas uninhabitable and their rehabilitation dangerous and extremely costly. What is the economics of a product that, for such a small investment, can produce such long-term suffering and depravation at such enormous cost?

Trade and the global economy

Economies are still managed on a national basis, yet global trade has become a significant driving force. While mechanisms such as the United Nations Conference on Trade and Development (UNCTAD) and the World Trade Organization (successor to the General Agree- ment on Tariffs and Trade – GATT) attempt to balance competing national self-interests, these are only the beginning of what will be required to manage trade from the perspective of the global economy.[4] In fact, most countries have not yet realized the full implications of the global market and find themselves caught between irreconcilable interests within their societies.

Economies are not simply statistical tables and accounts; they are driven by activities distributed in time and space. It is the spatial dimension that will become critical as we move towards an in- creasingly integrated world system. Resources, capacities and needs are not distributed evenly around the world. Some countries are rich in minerals or petroleum; others have prime agricultural areas; a few have little or nothing that is not more readily available somewhere else. Some areas are sparsely inhabited and have extensive resources still to be developed; others have dense but highly organized and productive societies; and still others are unable to meet even the basic needs of their rapidly expanding populations. There are differences in climate, geographic situation, cultural heritage and environmental vulnerability.

In the past, people had no way to compare their way of life or standard of living with others elsewhere, and this ignorance helped to maintain the status quo. Many did not know that they were poor until someone from outside came and told them, or they travelled to some wealthier area. Today the communications and transportation revolutions have physically tied all the planet together, and the concept of social justice which has already produced a considerable levelling of extremes of wealth and poverty in most industrialized countries will be invoked increasingly on a planetary scale. Trade and capital flows are mechanisms for reducing the natural and historical inequalities between countries. However, at present, they are accentuating the differences.

Our present world of protectionist measures, subsidies and export incentives is far from a global free market, with no trade barriers and a single currency, where each country would be able to develop its own comparative advantage in international commerce. The success strategy of every country today involves raising exports and lowering imports, a logical impossibility when everybody tries to do the same thing on a global scale. Industries that have saturated domestic markets must export if they are to continue to grow. Highly protected and subsidized agricultural sectors dump excess products overseas, undercutting the farmers in poor developing countries. Multinational corporations manipulate the varied national situations to their own profit without international controls.

The result today is serious imbalances in the global trading system, mostly to the advantage of the rich countries which can afford to shop around for the cheapest primary commodities and to subsidize production for dumping overseas. But even these countries have seen their traditional industries wither and fade, and suffer rising unemployment when their expensive labour cannot compete on the world market. The logic of the global free market appeals to industries with a technological advance which need larger markets and thus support the removal of tariff barriers to facilitate their expansion. But it runs headlong into the extreme differences in wealth and social welfare between countries, which a truly free market, allowed to operate without interference or manipulation, will try to equalize. With the rapidly expanding populations of poor countries providing an almost unlimited pool of cheap labour, the equalization will inevitably be downward, but the political stresses of trying to lower standards of living in rich countries where labour is well organized may be unbearable. It is these fundamental inconsistencies between free market forces and the gross inequalities between nations that will continue to stress the global trading system.

Similar stresses arise from environmental factors. The high environmental standards and strict controls on pollution, waste disposal and worker safety raise direct costs in the industrialized countries. Market forces therefore tend to push the most polluting industries to poor developing countries where environmental protection is lax if not entirely absent. The governments of these countries often welcome such investment, as any job creation is seen as better than the suffering of absolute poverty. Pollution controls are still often regarded as expensive luxuries. With free trade, the result again is pressure to lower environmental standards globally or to raise protectionist barriers, not to mention the growing environmental destruction and human health impacts in the industrial areas of poorer countries.[5]

World trade problems are made much worse by the continuing currency differences and variations between countries. Governments often adjust exchange rates to try to achieve trading advantages, such as by devaluing their currency to lower the price of their products in global markets. The considerable differences in prices of the same goods and services between countries are as much a reflection of differences in exchange rate as they are of real differences in costs. This can have a significant distorting effect on trade balances. Governments and central banks change interest rates, either to combat inflation, or to attract foreign capital to cover an expanding debt. All of these are then manipulated by speculators on the foreign currency markets who command sums that can overwhelm the capital reserves of many central banks. This is a recipe for continuing instability that ultimately benefits no one except the speculators.

International capital movements are another serious problem. The massive aid and commercial loan flows of the last fifty years to assist the least developed countries have often been used to support current consumption or for prestigious infrastructure. When a loan supports a productive project that generates revenues to reimburse the loan, this presents little difficulty, but the large number of ill-conceived and unsuccessful projects and the general waste and inefficiency have left a massive burden of financial debt that overwhelms poor countries already suffering from steadily worsening terms of trade. Much aid has also been in the form of military equipment or credits which make no productive contribution to the receiving economy. The problem is accentuated by capital flight, when those who do make money in developing countries but who lack confidence in the future of their countries export their capital for investment overseas. Corruption is also significant in many countries, with large sums destined for development being simply transferred to personal bank accounts overseas, leaving the country to service and reimburse the debt thus created. Even when a corrupt, extravagant or inefficient government is thrown out, the debt remains to burden its successors. Most countries try to honour their obligations in order to qualify for new loans, despite imposing enormous sacrifices on their populations in the name of structural adjustment. Since flows of new aid and loans are declining, there is a massive net transfer of capital from the poor countries to the rich as old loans and their accumulated interest are paid off. The poor are getting poorer, and the rich richer. Since the poor are in fact a significant proportion of humankind, the potential for instability and upheaval is as great today as it was in the age of the revolutions that overthrew monarchs and aristocracies.

Employment

One of the most glaring inconsistencies in present economic systems lies in the treatment of employment. A high value is placed on increases in productivity, which reduce the cost per unit of production. One of the major costs of production is labour, so reducing the labour input is highly desirable, and investments in computers, automation, robots and other labour-saving devices are an important way for industrialized countries with high wages and living standards to compete with developing countries where labour is cheap. The result, of course, is increasing unemployment in the rich countries. As productivity has risen in agriculture and industry, fewer and fewer people are needed to produce all the goods such countries can use. In the wealthiest countries, local markets eventually reach saturation for any particular product. Since it is hard to watch more than one television at a time, once everyone owns one (or even several in different rooms of the house), the only sales will be for the replacement of old models. Many industries must struggle to invent new products, or to cultivate new needs through advertising, in order to keep growing. Production for export is another solution, but this has other disadvantages, especially when everyone tries to do the same thing.

The philosopher Bertrand Russell gave the classic example of a factory producing all the pins a market could absorb. Then someone invents a machine that allows each worker to produce twice as many pins. Since no more pins can be sold, it might seem logical to allow each worker to work half as long for the same salary, but our present approach is to fire half the workers and increase profits and the salary of the other half in the name of increased productivity.

Modern economics has thus created a world at two speeds. Those within the wage economy earn salaries that make them good consumers of the products of the system. Because fewer and fewer people are needed for production, social welfare systems have been created in the wealthier countries to absorb some of the surplus people and give them the means of existence, making them good consumers also. Older experienced workers are retired on pensions to make room for new (and cheaper) recruits. Unemployment benefits help those thrown out of work to remain consumers a little longer. Education for the young is extended both to increase their usefulness and to keep them off the labour market as long as possible. As a result, an increasing proportion of the population is supported by such forms of charity financed by taxes and charges on wage-earners and corporations.

This process is encouraged in many countries where employers have little or no responsibility for former employees. Workers can be treated as goods, to be used while profitable, and then thrown away. Employment is privatized, but unemployment is a public responsibility. The development of service industries has helped absorb some of the surplus, but the pace of change has outdistanced the length of careers, and many people lack the necessary skills or are too old to move into these new sectors. Even from an economic perspective, the human wastage in such a situation is considerable and increasing, not to mention the social disruption and human suffering.

The problem is even more extreme in the poor developing countries of the Third World, where only a small, mostly urban elite are within the wage economy. The vast majority, both the urban unemployed and the rural subsistence population, are largely marginalized. A fortunate few may have a tiny cash income from trading, a cash crop or occasional employment, but often not enough even to meet basic needs, and generally spread over a large number of dependants. In many cases people starve to death not because there is no food, but because they have no money to buy food, and no way to earn such money.

The problems of poverty in the world are less in the total amount of available wealth than in the mechanisms for its distribution. As technology increases productivity, the present employment/wage system, tied to traditional economic activities, becomes less and less appropriate as a means of distributing wealth. A few work long hours for high salaries, others slave away at a pittance, while the rest, whose labour is no longer needed, live on charity or sink into poverty.

Thus the modern economic system in reality only serves a rich minority of the world population, with a significant fraction supported on charity or a subsistence income, and many largely excluded from participation. It seems ironic, if not tragic, that industrialized countries wallow in agricultural surpluses and under-utilized industrial capacity, and misuse their scientific and technical prowess, while the poor, both in the rich countries and in the developing world, represent an enormous potential demand, but lack the purchasing power to take advantage of the excess supply. To the observer uninitiated in the arcane ways of modern economics, this seems like a fundamental failure in the system.

Waste and pollution

Another inconsistency in the present economic system is the way it favours the externalization of costs and the internalization of benefits (i.e. somebody else bears the costs while you keep the profits). This is especially obvious in the area of environmental pollution. There is no fundamental structural mechanism to ensure that costs are borne by those responsible for them – often referred to as the 'polluter pays principle'. If an industry can simply dump its wastes in the environment without cost, it will do so. Only government regulations to protect the common good, or lawsuits by injured parties where this is possible, will make it do otherwise. Some enlightened industries are now cleaning up voluntarily, but often only to avoid the threat of regulation or to maintain a desirable market image. In many areas, government has to intervene to protect the long-term or more general interest of the public, because the economic value system favours short-term gain and penalizes 'unproductive' action for the public good.

The system also fails to hold industry responsible for the ultimate fate of its products, although this may now begin to change. When the amounts were small and waste disposal cheap, this did not seem to matter, but as the costs of disposal have risen in wealthy, densely populated countries, the problem of what to do with old automobiles, tyres and the increasing volumes of packaging, to name just a few problem wastes, has grown. The challenge is to adapt the economic system so that products reflect their full cost, not just of manufacture, but of their raw material extraction, social and environmental impact and ultimate disposal, in other words during their full life cycle from cradle to grave. Many of the problems with the present economic system are due to its failure to provide mechanisms to reflect and internalize the full costs of economic activities.

The problem of wastes and toxic materials and their environmental impacts is particularly evident when it comes to sharing costs between the present and future generations. In simple terms, this means making money now, and leaving someone else (i.e. our children or grandchildren) to clean up the mess later. Already, many developed countries are discovering thousands of old industrial sites contaminated with hazardous materials since the beginning of the industrial revolution, and now requiring expensive clean-up, often at public expense. The situation is more widespread than is generally realized. The damage to the stratospheric ozone layer, and the threat of global warming from greenhouse gases, are other examples of future costs from past (and present) accumulations of wastes. There are also the 'chemical time bombs' represented by chemicals, perhaps widely used in agriculture or industry and deposited in the soil, that are now slowly filtering down into the ground water, which they may seriously contaminate and render unfit for human consumption in a few decades, leaving us helpless to do much about it. The problem of nuclear materials is another example. Plutonium and other radioactive materials and wastes manufactured over the last half century may require careful and expensive management for hundreds or thousands of years to keep them totally isolated from humans and other living things, yet the costs of that management are seldom considered in the economic assessments of the nuclear industry. Added together, all these factors suggest that we have already seriously mortgaged the future of coming generations with our short-sightedness.

Dominance of the short term

Economists do have a way of representing such future costs. It is called discounting, and is one of the more controversial and arbitrary elements in modern economics. It is basically the percentage by which a future value is reduced for each intervening year to determine its present value. It is often based on the present cost of borrowing money. In practice, its use usually means that any cost more than one or at the most a few decades into the future is considered insignificant.

The linkage of discounting to present interest rates is part of the problem. Interest rates are related to short-term economic prospects and to rates of inflation, which are odd criteria for measuring the importance of the distant future. Interest is also an important motor for what we, today, call economic growth. We take it as natural that money must grow, yet in the longer term compounding interest at today's rates leads to economic absurdities.[6]

This illustrates another weakness in the present economic system, in that it favours the short term over the long term. There is little economic incentive to invest for future generations, or to forego the use of resources because they may be needed later. For instance, reforestation projects favour fast-growing trees to produce a quick return on investment. Economic calculations argue against planting slower-growing hardwoods, which may produce the most valuable timber and the greatest ecological services, but which will take eighty to one hundred and fifty years to reach a harvestable size. No investor wants to wait that long to profit from his investment. There is thus a strong bias in present methods against long-term planning. For an economist, long-term means looking twenty years into the future. Economics deals very poorly with the dimension of time, both because of methodological problems such as discounting, and because investors, politicians and other clients of economists want rapid pay-offs. This emphasis on short-term bottom-line results is now built in to the Western system of corporate ownership and governance; the managers of pension and mutual funds, who control much investment capital, will push to replace any chief executive officer who does not show continued improvement in quarterly earnings. There has thus been no incentive to develop a chronoeconomics, or economics of time. Sustainability requires a consideration of the future, but over what time period? This is one of the problems with defining sustainable development. Until long-term planning becomes integrated into economic and social management, we shall continue to pile a variety of kinds of debt on future generations. The morality of this practice is dubious, to say the least.

Growth

One of the most entrenched values in the present economic paradigm is the way it favours growth as an absolute good. An industry or economy that is not growing is considered unsuccessful; more growth is the solution to all our economic problems. The suggestion in the report sponsored in the early 1970s by the Club of Rome[7] that there might be limits to growth was seen in many circles as anathema. Admittedly there are many poor whose needs must be met, and many other reasons to encourage further growth in available resources and goods to achieve development, but ultimately material growth cannot continue forever in a closed system, and the planet is a closed system.[8]

One could easily point to absurd limits to growth, such as the population growing until every bit of land had someone standing on it, or highway construction continuing until all the land was paved. More realistically, how much growth in television sales is possible once everyone already has one? There will be some replacement sales for those that wear out, and to some consumers who can be convinced to have one in each room of the house, but sooner or later saturation will be reached, apart from new demand created by changing technology, or by population growth, which itself must ultimately stop. Limits are equally evident for growth in the production of toxic and persistent materials that accumulate in the environment, and which will ultimately reach a concentration dangerous for people and other life. One could add an argument of substitutability, admitting that growth in any one product can be limited, but that there are endless possibilities to substitute one product for another and thus to maintain overall growth in the economy. However, this assumes that individual consumers will never reach saturation in their acquisition of material goods, and that resources are available in endless quantities to produce such goods. Neither assumption is tenable. Consumption does reach a point of diminishing returns unless turnover is increased through reduced durability or intentional destruction, as in warfare. Most estimates suggest that resources on the planet are insufficient to provide every living person with the same standard of living as that of the well-off American or European. Los Angeles has enough automobiles for everyone to sit in the front seats. What would the same density of vehicles and roads do to land use and food production in Bangladesh?

There may already be specific fields today where growth in certain activities, with negative effects, may no longer be desirable, at least in some regions. Scenic areas may need to limit tourism development to prevent destruction of the very assets that attract the tourists. Growth in fertilizer use ultimately reaches the limit of the crop to respond, and may increase short-term production at the expense of long-term sustainability of the soil and clean water. We can reach environmental saturation, or even over-shoot critical limits, damaging the future capacity of the planet. Thus the concept of growth must no longer be seen as a general good and automatically desirable, even a right that must be respected; it needs to be defined more selectively with respect to specific social aims, values and limits in time and space.

For many people, growth and development are synonymous, yet growth can even be counter-productive to real development, and development can include qualitative changes that do not require growth. The two processes need to be distinguished clearly and managed accordingly. The economic growth of the industrialized countries over the last few decades has not, in fact, led to any proportional increase in the quality of life.[9]

Planetary limits will eventually require our civilization to achieve a steady state in both population size and economic activities. Material growth will ultimately only be possible to the extent that increases in efficiency and productivity within the limitations of the global environment permit. This is a fact grounded in the objective nature of physical reality, just as you cannot add any more water to an already full glass without it running over. Any idea to the contrary is wishful thinking, if not a blatant disregard for scientific facts. The reason why any thought of an end to growth is anathema in political, economic and business circles is that Western capitalism as preached today cannot survive without growth.[10] In the present system, businesses and national economies must expand or collapse.

Rates of growth

Another aspect of growth that needs to be studied with care is the rate of growth. Many things can grow geometrically, which means that as they double and double and then double again, the numbers begin to increase astronomically. The human population has been growing this way, with the time for each doubling getting shorter and shorter. This means that where there are absolute limits, and on our planet there must be sooner or later, we could approach them very rapidly. In the classic example of water lilies in a pond doubling the area they cover every day, it will take many days before a quarter of the pond is covered, but then only two more for it to be covered completely. It is thus not only the absolute amounts of growth, but also the rates of growth that need to be looked at very carefully as we try to plan for our future. The economic system, with its short-term perspective, is very poorly adapted to anticipate or deal with this kind of phenomenon.

There is often an assumption in economic and political circles that science and technology will find a solution to any problem. There have been doom-mongers in the past, and yet we seem to have avoided, so far, the Malthusian crunch. The human race has demonstrated an enormous survival capacity, a couple of world wars not withstanding. There is clearly still great potential in our powers of invention, and it would be foolhardy to suggest that we can predict the planet's ultimate human carrying capacity or the limits to human ingenuity. At present, it is probably more appropriate to ask if we can cope with the accelerating rates of change. The human lifespan is extending, not contracting, making it harder to keep up. The shortening turnover time for industrial technologies may be outdistancing our ability to raise the capital for new investments while increasing the costs to write off the old technologies, not to mention trying to adapt the labour force to the new requirements and making the necessary social adjustments. The stresses this is placing on our economy and society are considerable.

Part of the problem is due to the different scales and paces of growth between human activities, which we can control, and the natural world, where rates are beyond our influence and scales can exceed our capacity to respond. The speed with which chemicals move in the environment and are detoxified or recycled by natural processes, or that a biological resource is able to regenerate after harvesting, cannot necessarily be accelerated. One could imagine a technology to filter pollutants out of the ambient air or from ocean water, but could it ever be applied on a large enough scale to have a significant effect? In addition, there are often long time lags between a cause and a visible effect, such that damage may become apparent, and the true costs evident, only long after the causative act. The faster the rate of growth, the greater the danger of over-shooting limits or of not identifying damage until far too late. The problems in the asbestos industry illustrate this well, where the ten to twenty-year delay between asbestos exposure in workers and the appearance of asbestosis and lung cancer allowed the industry to accumulate an enormous liability in workers' compensation, not to mention the human suffering, before the dangers became evident.

Power and money

Money and power have mingled since the two were invented, and the abuse of that combination for selfish interest is probably one of society's most ancient problems. Among international economic activities, the arms trade and the illicit drugs trade rank up with the petroleum industry in importance. Given the power of money, especially where corruption is rife in so many political systems, the moral implications of this are frightening. The scale of international financial flows has grown so large as to escape any control, with even the central banks of the most powerful countries collectively helpless before institutional investors in search of the best short-term return and less scrupulous speculators out for a quick dollar, not to mention multinationals trying to avoid taxes and crime syndicates laundering money.

This has become, in fact, a highly significant threat to the national security and well-being of most countries, particularly the richest, with the poorest in fact the least vulnerable because they have little to lose. What is the use of national sovereignty where whole states can be bought off by special interests? Organized crime, in particular, is accumulating enormous economic power which will certainly not be used for the collective benefit of humankind.

Governments are especially vulnerable to the weight of economic interests, both through legitimate lobbying and through bribery and corruption. The opportunities and temptations are everywhere. Politics is increasingly becoming the art of trying to satisfy the largest number of wealthy pressure groups. Political success depends on the benefits returned to the constituency – what the Americans call pork-barrel politics. Even in democratic electoral systems, votes can be bought, not necessarily directly but through the financing of expensive mass-media electoral campaigns, public relations and image-making. This inevitably favours the views of the wealthy, and leaves the poor disenfranchised. Under such conditions, there is little or no motivation to govern in the larger public interest, particularly if the long-term benefits require short-term costs.

Political and economic interests have become extensively interlocked, so that government is in many ways an extension of business. In some countries the same small clique provides both leaders and investors; in others, it is normal to move between government and the boards of major corporations. We are accustomed to seeing heads of government travel to foreign countries with a suite of corporate executives and high-level salespeople out to land lucrative contracts.

Economic influence is also evident in the use of much development aid for political ends and commercial advantages. Many countries use aid primarily in their own self-interest, to open or preserve markets and to help national industries. There are many trade-offs between aid packages and other foreign-policy objectives, and much aid is tied to purchases from donor-country suppliers.

It must be emphasized that the above litany of economic faults should not lead to the implication that all the basic principles of modern economics or democratic government are wrong. It is their completeness and application that often leave something to be desired, and their inability at present to cope with other important dimensions of human society. This problem will be addressed in the chapters that follow.

Notes

1. This idea has been developed by Fritjof Capra in *The Turning Point* and *Uncommon Wisdom*.

2. Russell (1994).

3. UNDP, *Human Development Report 1995*. This annual report is one of the best attempts to explore what development means in human as opposed to economic terms.

4. See, for instance, my short discussion presented at a 1994 GATT Symposium on Trade, Environment and Sustainable Development in Dahl (1994b) 'Global Sustainability and its Implications for Trade'.

5. Ibid.

6. Russell (1994).

7. Meadows et al. (1972).
8. Hardin (1991).
9. Douthwaite (1992).
10. Russell (1994).

CHAPTER 3

Where are we going?

The need for a more comprehensive and integrated approach to the planning and management of human civilization can be illustrated by a summary of some of the principal components of our social, economic and environmental systems and the implications for the future of present trends in these components.

Population

The dominant trend, among all those which have recently marked and will continue for some time to come to mark our society, is the phenomenal growth in both human population and in levels of per-capita consumption. While projections differ depending on a variety of assumptions, estimates suggest that the world will have to find space, resources and means of livelihood for some 9 to 14 billion (thousand million) people by the middle of the twenty-first century, that is, within the lifetimes of children living today. This means that the world will be approximately twice as crowded as it is today, and will require twice the present consumption of resources, even assuming no improvement in the living standards of the vast numbers of the poor. It also assumes that the birth rate will decline to replacement level, leading to the stabilization of population size during that period. The former assumption is morally unacceptable, and the latter perhaps overly optimistic, unless the death rate rises catastrophically. Several dimensions of this problem need to be considered, including the rate of growth, the level of consumption, the distribution of people relative to resources, the total sustainable population (carrying capacity) of the planet, and the implications of such crowding on our well-being and quality of life.

Many of the most acute problems associated today with population growth result, in fact, from the rate of growth. Each human being requires food, housing, schooling, employment, health care and other resources and facilities in varying proportions at different times in life. In a stable population, the generations replace each

29

other. Individuals advance in school or in their occupations, but are replaced by equal numbers of others so that the requirement for facilities and jobs remains constant. However, in a growing population, there is a continuing need for new school-rooms and teachers, more water supply, increased land for food production, additional housing, new jobs, and all the other things that people require. These involve a significant capital investment and growth in human institutions. When the population grows more rapidly than the society can afford to invest in all these things, then the existing social infrastructure must accommodate more people, diluting the amount per person and reducing the average quality of life. If there is an unequal distribution of resources in the society, the rich and powerful will maintain their living standards, but the number of poor will increase. The highest population growth rates today are in the disadvantaged populations and in the poorest countries, which can least afford to invest. The result is mushrooming urban slums filled with those desperate for a better life, and an increasing number of rural landscapes degraded by those who had neither the chance to learn how nor the means to manage them wisely as their numbers outstripped the capacity of traditional systems. Even in wealthy countries with lower population growth rates but higher per-capita consumption rates, providing more housing, transport, employment, recreation, waste disposal, etc., requires a considerable effort.

The numbers of people cannot be considered in isolation from their rates of consumption of resources. A single individual in an industrialized country may consume two hundred times the resources of one in a poor country, and thus have a proportionately larger impact on the environment. Thus, even a small population increase in a wealthy country can be much more significant in terms of global impact than a higher increase among the poor.

When rapid growth is followed by rapid stabilization due to a sharp decline in the birth rate, as has happened in some countries, another problem emerges. Most social welfare systems depend on revenues from the working population to support the elderly, for whom social services and medical expenses can be very high. If, because of changing birth rates, the number of aged is large and a smaller work force is left to support them, then a crisis in social welfare will result.

The distribution of the population increase is equally significant. Most of the projected growth in population will occur in the developing countries which are generally least able to cope with the increase, and often in resource-poor areas where the additional population will degrade fragile resources. While it might seem logical to move excess populations to wealthier countries which have the resources to support them, any discussion of such population movements between countries seems to be anathema. Free movement of goods, and of capital, are encouraged, but not the free movement of people. Industrialized countries worried about a declining birth rate may offer fiscal incentives to have more children, but they would never consider filling depopulated rural villages with excess Chinese or Africans.

Under-capitalized population growth, where the necessary investment has not been made to make people productive members of society with their basic needs fulfilled, accumulates another kind of debt. Most societies accept the obligation to educate children and to give everyone opportunities for employment and self-advancement. Such principles are enshrined in the universal declarations of human rights. These investments in human capital are seen as essential for social and political stability in advanced democratic societies. Each person who is uneducated or under-educated, who is poorly housed or under-employed, represents so much under-capitalized, and therefore under-utilized, potential that will require a considerable investment to provide the opportunities and quality of life now considered normal in industrialized countries. The difference between that person's actual state of ignorance and poverty, and the state of education and well-being to which he or she should have a right as a human being, is as much an accumulation of debt as the loans that most countries must repay to foreign creditors. Today, we are equally likely to default on both kinds of debt.

Given such rapid population growth on a planet that is ultimately finite, and our present inability to meet even the basic needs of much of the world's population, the human carrying capacity of the Earth has become a significant issue. The carrying capacity of a bus is the total number of people that it can carry without it becoming dangerously overcrowded or unsafe. Similarly, the world's carrying capacity is the number of people that can live on it without dangerously threatening its future.

The idea of carrying capacity relates closely to that of sustainable development, because both refer to living off income rather than capital. Consider a retired person living on the interest from a small investment account which produces just enough to cover basic expenses. He can increase his standard of living by dipping into the capital, but this will reduce future income. Spending all the money in the account in a big splurge will mean nothing left for the future. The human population of the planet faces a similar situation. If we cut down forests faster than they can grow back, intensify agriculture until it robs the soil of its fertility, and make profligate use of non-renewable resources such as minerals and fossil fuels, we can increase our standard of living and/or the number of people living here, but we reduce the capacity of the world to support people in the future. The richest countries may feel, on the basis of their national experience, that their development can go on for ever, but they fail to realize that their wealth has come partly from diminishing stocks of non-renewable resources, and partly from the import of cheap primary commodities often produced by over-exploitation in developing countries, just as the empires of earlier times flourished through colonial exploitation. Much development in the West was fuelled by expansion into new frontiers, which provided a safety valve for social pressures. In today's increasingly crowded world, new frontiers are few and far between, and there are no alternative safety valves for our excesses. Any student of history can find many examples of the rapid rise and fall of wealthy societies.

It is difficult to estimate the carrying capacity of the planet, since this depends on the technologies available, our efficiency in the use of resources, and the standard of living we will accept. Since the richest one-fifth of the population today uses about four-fifths of the world's resources, the existing world population could not be brought up to, say, European living standards using present technologies and consumption levels. Pessimists will thus say that the world is already over-populated, and that the future population must be reduced to achieve sustainability. Optimists assume that science and technology will find solutions to all our problems so that growth can go on for ever. The predictions in the early 1970s of limits to growth and a collapse in civilization[1] have not yet been realized, but the same group now says that we are beyond the limits, cushioned only by the time lags between cause and effect, and that unless we draw back quickly, their dire predictions will still come true.[2] Predicting the future is a most hazardous occupation; the clever only predict so far into the future that they will not be around to see if their predictions are right or wrong. However, common sense shows that the present situation of runaway population growth, massive over-exploitation of resources and steady accumulation of pollution and wastes cannot continue. The question is how and by what means change will come, and how much damage to the natural capital and carrying capacity of the planet we shall do in the process.

Another dimension of the population problem is the implication of increased crowding for human well-being and quality of life. Experiments with caged colonies of rats show that increased crowding leads to many forms of aggressive and deviant behaviour, not unlike those observed in many urban areas. Megacities are growing explosively all over the world, and the percentage of the population living in cities is steadily rising. The possibilities of accessible peace and quiet, wilderness and solitude are shrinking rapidly. People are continuing to crowd in cities at the same time that new technologies of communications and transportation are making it less and less necessary to be in physical proximity in order to carry out the business of the modern world. The concentration of pollution and wastes, the spread of diseases due to overcrowding, the time wasted in long commutes and traffic jams, the nervous stress from noise, crime, and over-saturated senses, all reduce the quality of life in what may best be described as an over-developed civilization. With projected future population growth, the prospects are not good.

Non-renewable resources

Many of the resources required by our present civilization are non-renewable, that is they occur in a limited quantity on this planet and once used are not replaced. This is particularly true of fossil fuels, which are discussed under energy below, and of mineral resources such as metals. Some metals, such as iron, occur in soils in such high concentrations that there is no fear of exhausting them, but others (copper, chrome, nickel, gold, etc.) are found in ores with economically extractable concentrations in only a few locations. As mineral prospecting becomes more thorough and intensive around the world, the chance of new discoveries declines. The highest-grade ore bodies are being mined out, requiring the use of ever poorer ores or those in less accessible locations where extraction costs are higher. While prices may fluctuate due to short-term variations in supply and demand, the long-term trend is inevitably towards increasing costs of production and transport. However, as prices rise, the pressure increases to replace these materials with cheaper substitutes. Thus we shall probably never 'run out' of any of these resources, but to the extent that our civilization continues to depend on them, the cost of maintaining the same level of consumption will rise inexorably. Even standing still will cost more. Spreading the limited supply among more people will raise the price even further.

Recycling is one option that is being considered increasingly for such resources. As prices rise, it becomes more economic to recover and reuse metals rather than to extract them from the earth. To the extent that we can close the loop or the 'life cycle' of such materials, we make their use sustainable in the long term. For essential uses, for which substitutes cannot be found, this is our only option.

The picture is complicated by changes in demand caused by changes in technology. Lead was once widely used in water pipes. Its major use as a fuel additive, tetra-ethyl lead, is now being phased out. If new battery technologies replace the lead-acid battery, the demand could drop sharply. It is thus difficult to predict which non-renewable resources could become most limiting. Some predict that phosphorus for use as fertilizer could become a constraint as high-grade phosphate deposits are exhausted, seriously handicapping agricultural production. It is hard to see how technology can find a substitute for a basic plant nutrient.

Many resources such as soils, forests and ground water, that in theory are renewable, are in fact being treated today as non-renewable resources on any reasonable time scale and are being driven to exhaustion. This issue is discussed in more detail below.

Energy

Energy is perhaps the most essential resource for civilization, whether as food energy for ourselves or as the power to magnify human effort, manufacture what we need, drive our transport and communications, and modify our environment and life-style to our liking. While energy comes in many forms that can often be substituted for each other, it ultimately comes from two sources, the renewable energy from the sun, or non-renewable sources within the planet. The former includes the energy captured in plants (wood and food crops); the energy of falling water (hydroelectricity) driven by solar evaporation in the water cycle; wind, wave and ocean thermal energy from solar heating; and the direct use of solar energy for electricity generation or water-heating. Non-renewable energy sources include the energy from radioactive decay, whether naturally in geothermal energy or artificially in nuclear fission or fusion reactions, as well as the fossil fuels which contain solar energy from ancient biological activity stored by geological processes.

Western civilization depends to an overwhelming extent on fossil fuels as the prime energy source for industry, transport and urban life. While competition among oil producing countries to keep their incomes up has led to an oversupply and lower prices, and some countries are making progress in increasing energy efficiency, global projections are for an ever-increasing demand. If consumption stays high or grows, known oil reserves are projected to last less than a century. Coal reserves are more important, particularly in China, but the environmental costs of mining and burning coal are very high. The release of carbon dioxide from fossil fuel consumption is threatening to change the climate in coming decades with unpredictable and possibly disastrous consequences for many inhabited areas.

We must find alternative energy sources before the increasing scarcity of fossil fuels drives prices to insupportable levels, and possibly much sooner if we are to prevent massive climate change and the attendant consequences. Yet there is an enormous inertia built into our industrial society's addiction to fossil fuels. The costs of writing off and replacing our massive investments in present energy systems are almost unthinkably large and, in addition, there are powerful vested interests against change. We have built a civilization on cheap energy from highly concentrated sources; but having lived off this particular capital, we now face higher costs and lower benefits in the future. The inevitable reduction in material standards of living will increase social stresses in the wealthy countries that benefited the most, while poor countries are experiencing the frustration of seeing their dreams of Western-style development evaporate.

Nuclear energy is often proposed as an almost inexhaustible alternative. However, even the most technically advanced countries have not found a permanent solution for the long-term disposal of radioactive wastes. The economics of nuclear energy are highly dubious, because they include neither the enormous subsidies that came from the military development of nuclear science, nor the expenses of safely decommissioning nuclear power plants and the long-term storage of nuclear wastes. Once radioactive materials are produced, they are so dangerous that they must be kept totally isolated, at great expense, from all forms of life and thus from the whole planetary environment. Some disintegrate quickly, but others will remain dangerous for a long time. Plutonium will have to be kept in completely safe storage for 10,000 to 20,000 years, longer than any civilization has ever existed. While some experiments are now beginning to see if such materials can be consumed in further nuclear reactions, it has yet to be demonstrated that this will actually reduce the quantity of dangerous nuclear wastes.

The manufacture of radioactive materials, and of other toxic and persistent chemicals, is another burden of expense or debt that we are placing on future generations. Our descendants will be required to divert part of their wealth from productive uses to protecting themselves from, or cleaning up, this lethal heritage, and their standard of living will be reduced accordingly. Already our present generation is having to bear the costs of cleaning up toxic waste dumps, contaminated industrial sites and other burdens which our parents and grandparents, in their ignorance or selfish short-sightedness, have left for us.

The conversion to renewable energy sources in industrialized countries has already begun. Solar water heating is already well established in some regions. Wind-generated electricity is now commercially viable. Solar cells provide electricity to many remote installations where the costs of connecting to a grid are too high. Biomass, often from agricultural or forestry waste, is used to generate electricity where it is readily available in large enough quantities. However, this conversion will lead to more than just a replacement of one technology by another. Renewable energy sources are diffuse and distributed over large areas, like sunlight itself. Their availability is thus the reverse of most present energy sources, which are concentrated in large power plants, mines, wells and refineries, with the energy then distributed over electric grids or as transportable fuels. While past energy availability has been one of the driving forces for urban and industrial concentration, as well as being a controlling factor in transport technologies, the rising cost of fossil fuels and the shift to diffuse renewable energy sources and fuels will encourage a reverse trend towards widespread, low-density development. The energy transition may help to bring a restructuring of society as we know it.

Renewable resources

One of the consequences of both the growing human population and the rising resource consumption of the rich has been increasing pressure on renewable resources. The original natural endowment of the planet included vast forests that generated rich and productive soils in many temperate lands. These have become the major agricultural areas of the world, and some of them have been cultivated for centuries. However, the drive for ever-higher productivity and profit in agriculture has brought increasing chemical fertilizer and pesticide use, large-scale mechanization and soil clearing with its risk of erosion, reduced fallow or other soil regeneration techniques, the spread of irrigation with its potential for salt accumulation or waterlogging, and other changes that are collectively threatening long-term agricultural productivity. Farmers today are often pushed to mine the soil the way we mine minerals. The same thing is happening to forest resources, where the global rate of cutting and clearing far exceeds the rate of replanting and regeneration. Corporate farming and forestry, in particular, may treat the land like any other industrial investment; if it yields, say, sixty years of profit until it is fully depreciated and written off, it is considered a good investment.

The problem of another renewable resource, ocean fisheries, is a further illustration of our short-sightedness. Fish are what is referred to as a common resource, belonging to no one in particular and available for anyone to catch. It is in the interest of each fisherman to catch as many fish as possible, because if he does not, someone else will. Each will therefore invest in larger boats and nets as long as this is profitable, until the over-capacity in the fishing fleet exceeds the potential of the fishery and everyone loses money, so that investment stops. Most ocean fisheries are in this state today, with debt-burdened fishermen trying to pay off their investments from diminishing catches in over-fished waters. Globally, catches exceed the sustainable yields determined by the UN Food and Agriculture Organization, and many fisheries are in decline, if not complete collapse. Such a situation has been called the 'tragedy of the commons', and can only be corrected by limiting access to the resource so that those who use it have a motivation to manage it sustainably.

The consequence of the destruction of renewable resources, and the lack of adequate investment in the replanting of forests, the regeneration of soils and the restoration of depleted fish stocks, is what can be called an accumulating resource debt resulting from the draw-down of the planet's natural resource capital. As the planet's non-renewable resource base shrinks, the future of civilization will depend more and more on the restoration of the productive capacity of these renewable resources, but this will require massive investments to correct decades of neglect.

There are many examples, particularly in the Mediterranean basin and the Middle East, of dry and stony lands that once supported great civilizations, which collapsed when they had exhausted their forests and soils. A tragic lesson in microcosm is that of Easter Island, an isolated volcanic island in the South Pacific that was colonized by Polynesian voyagers. A rich society developed, able to carve and erect giant stone statues across the island. But as the population grew, the forest was cleared and the island could no longer support so many people. However, since all the trees had been cut, it was impossible to build canoes to sail away. Wars broke out, and the population had already shrunk to a shadow of its former self by the time European explorers came into contact with the island.

One special kind of resource, whose value we are only beginning to appreciate, is the rich biological diversity with which millions of years of evolution have endowed the earth. Since it is biological activity that made the planet habitable originally, the maintenance of the life-support systems on which we depend requires the continued health of the vast biological systems on land and in the sea. Now that human impacts have for the first time reached a planetary scale, the richness, diversity and stability of these living systems is at risk. Species are being driven to extinction at an ever-increasing rate, just when the explosion of knowledge in genetics and biotechnology is giving us the tools to tap and use the rich genetic diversity of natural systems. Efforts are now being made through the new biodiversity convention and other measures to stem the tide of destruction, but again the inertia of expanding populations in a desperate drive for survival and development, combined with cynical exploitation by some of the unscrupulous rich and powerful, will make it difficult to save a major part of our biological heritage from extinction.

The land is in many ways our most precious resource. It is our home, our granary, and ultimately our tomb. Yet we all too seldom respect it, care for it, and use it wisely. Because many human settlements started as agricultural centres and market towns, much urban growth has taken place on the most productive agricultural land. As the best land is degraded or converted to unproductive uses, we are forced to develop more marginal lands, which will be more expensive to maintain and where costs per unit of output will be higher. Here, again, it will cost ever more to stand still, and the ultimate result will be a declining standard of living. This may not seem important in countries where agricultural surpluses and high-cost agricultural systems are forcing large areas out of production, but globally agricultural productivity is now rising more slowly than population growth, and we could too easily reach the point where there is just not enough food left on the planet to keep everyone alive.

Part of the problem is that the interests of the individual land-owner do not always coincide with the larger public good. Even the most profitable agricultural uses cannot compete with the profits to be made from urban land development. Yet in a rational land-use policy, where the land resource is allocated to its highest potential use in the interests of a sustainable future, the best soils should be reserved for intensive agriculture, poorer soils allocated to grazing, and steeper slopes to forestry, with housing, industry and urban development concentrated largely on stony or otherwise unusable land. The misuse of land is another aspect of resource debt which will become important as the human population approaches the carrying capacity of countries, continents and ultimately the planet.

The human environment

Human beings are diverse and adaptable creatures, but it is still amazing how little attention has been given to organizing and design-ing our own human environment to meet our requirements. We crowd into megacities where life sometimes seems to approach traditional descriptions of hell. (If Dante were alive today, he would certainly find new sources of inspiration for Inferno in urban air pollution, slums and traffic jams.) The vast housing projects that have had to be razed twenty years after construction because they were unlivable shows how wrong we can be. Monuments to urban grandeur leave people feeling dwarfed and insignificant. Computer-managed buildings take away any possibility to control your own environment. Patterns of living and working are so disrupted that all sense of community is lost. The time lost in travel between home and work is subtracted from time with the family, reducing the quality of family life. Most cities have gone far beyond any economies of scale, such that it may be much more expensive to maintain a person at a certain standard of living in a city than in a more rural area. It is hard to find corresponding benefits that could not also be provided by other smaller-scale systems of social organ-ization.

With too much crowding, too many encounters with people, and the bombardment of the media, people suffer from information overload and must adopt defensive mechanisms. The quality of human contacts is degraded. People who are unable to relate to their spouses, their parents or their children may turn to television or the cinema to experience vicariously all those emotions lacking in their real life. The automobile is a particularly appealing form of transportation in Western culture, in part because it is a protection against unwanted encounters, a little bit of home in which to feel secure while travelling door to door, and often a symbol of our pretensions, a new armour to protect us from an inner vulnerability.

Western society may be technologically advanced, but it is peopled by psychological and social barbarians, unaware of how to build a human environment that uplifts rather than degrades the human spirit. We have not learned what sorts of physical environments encourage social contacts and a sense of community, and reduce stress and conflict. Yet it should be possible to help communities to grow organically in ways that are enriching for all their members.

One critical dimension is that of the size or scale of communities. How many people is it possible to meet and feel comfortable with? How can we maximize enriching human contacts? What is the optimal size to support economic, cultural and recreational opportunities? How do we avoid the diseconomies of large urban size? In one study to determine the best size for a university, it was decided that the ideal student population was 14,000, because this allowed for maximum diversity of opportunities while keeping individual departments to a scale allowing full scholarly interchange and also avoided the need to start duplicating library resources. Similar approaches could be used to rethink the way we scale many human institutions and communities.

Technologies

Much modern development is conditioned by our transportation systems. Compare villages scaled to foot traffic, cities which grew up when the horse was the principal mode of transport, and the suburban sprawl that has resulted from reliance on the automobile. Older cities are now so choked by vehicular traffic that they are having to exclude the automobile and revert to pedestrian malls and public transport in city centres. In transportation as in many other fields, we are caught in the inertia of our present way of doing things, unable to change despite the inefficiencies that have often resulted from a good thing carried too far.

Given the Western psychological and physical dependence on the automobile, it is difficult to imagine abandoning it in the near future in those countries that have invested so heavily in it. One option would be to redesign the automobile so that its passenger and baggage compartment was detachable from the motor and chassis, allowing the connection of the passenger compartment to various propulsion systems. This would allow the same vehicle to connect to high-density computer-controlled electric propulsion systems in cities, high-speed mass-transit convoys between cities, and individual petroleum- or bio-fuelled motors for low-density rural travel, with rapid interchange at appropriate transfer points. The increased flexibility in the technology would allow a considerable reduction in environmental impact and permit the more effective redesign of human communities. However, this would require a level of co-operation among auto manufacturers, mass-transit companies, the energy industry and governments that may be difficult to achieve at present. The global imposition of the automobile as a standard technology is also inappropriate. For instance, small tropical islands need a vehicle able to carry a family of ten no more than 50 km at a speed of 40 km per hour, a need better met by a solar-powered or wind-recharged electric plastic vehicle than a standard automobile over-engineered for the local environment and rusting out in less than two years of sea wind and salt spray. Much more flexibility and imagination are needed in meeting the world's varied transport needs.

Our compartmentalized and fragmented approach to technological civilization threatens our human environment in other ways. Anyone today can invent a new product, whether mechanical, chemical or electronic, and put it on the market. In the advanced countries, many unfortunate experiences have led to increasing requirements for safety and consumer protection, and more recently for reduced environmental impact, but this is largely on a national (or in Europe, regional) basis. Many products that are banned or restricted at home can still be freely exported and sold in countries with much less capacity to protect their populations. Furthermore, there are no effective mechanisms to examine threatened impacts on a world-wide basis and to regulate the global manufacture and use of threatening products. There are a number of persistent and toxic chemicals, for instance, such as PCBs and some pesticides, that are becoming planetary pollution problems. The one successful case where a global ban is now being applied is for chemicals which are damaging the stratospheric ozone layer, where an international legal agreement was laboriously negotiated by the wealthy manufacturing countries, and then a fund established to assist the poorer countries to adhere to it.

Wastes

There is also too little examination of the effects of a product once it is used, and the result is the mountains of waste that are becoming increasingly expensive to dispose of, and rising levels of chemical pollution whose future consequences are only dimly perceived. Often the environment can only absorb safely or purify some limited quantity of chemicals or wastes. Moderate activities within these limits show little or no environmental effect, and we may blithely continue increasing our activity until suddenly the environmental capacity is exceeded and major impacts occur. By this time, the industrial inertia and established consumer habits may make controlling the activity a long and expensive process, during which time much more damage is done. There must be many ways in which our short-sightedness, ignorance or wilful disregard of the risks will result in unpleasant surprises in the future, creating another burden of debt that those who follow us will have to pay.

The damage to the ozone layer by halocarbon compounds is one of the first clear examples of human impact on an important global process that risks causing significant global health and environmental damage. Control measures have been implemented, but because of the long time lags in large-scale global systems, it may be a century before the problem is overcome, and in the meantime the damage could be considerable.

The threat of global warming and climate change resulting from the increase in 'greenhouse gases' such as carbon dioxide from fossil fuel combustion and methane from agriculture, livestock and natural gas leaks (among other sources), is an even more complex problem. There is considerable scientific uncertainty as to the size and timing of any effects, but recent research shows that climate can be quite unstable and can change significantly over decades. A major climate shift could seriously alter the agricultural productivity and carrying capacity of whole regions, creating enormous costs for adaptation and pressures for massive population shifts with a high potential for conflict. Yet any attempt to reduce our production of greenhouse gases significantly (reductions of 60–80 per cent may be required) would mean writing off gigantic investments in industry and infra-structure, developing new technological foundations for civilization and restructuring economies, with significant shifts in comparative advantage between countries and regions, all of which are being resisted by powerful forces in society.

Poverty

Many of the above problems are those of wealth and over-consumption. There is an equally large range of problems associated with the plight of the poor, especially those in developing countries. Poverty reduces or eliminates choices; desperation leaves little room for the option of avoiding risks or reducing long-term consequences. Survival must come first. In some parts of the world, population growth and migrations, environmental degradation and diminishing resources are pushing people from subsistence life-styles that were in approximate balance with their environment, over the edge into the vicious circles of overcrowding, malnutrition and unacceptable water, housing and sanitation that define absolute poverty.

The combination of high population densities, poor hygiene and sanitation, inadequate medical care, accumulating resistance in pathogens and insect vectors, and high mobility are increasing our global vulnerability to epidemics. The annual cycles of influenza show how easily diseases are spread around the world. Today there are growing risks both from new diseases like AIDS and from old ones that are now making a comeback, like malaria, cholera, yellow fever and tuberculosis. For these, it is the widespread occurrence of poverty, allowing such diseases to gather a momentum, which puts everyone, rich or poor, at risk.

There is no way that the problems of poverty can be separated from those of the environment and sustainable development. Eliminating poverty is an essential prerequisite at the global level for progress in other areas. The prevalence of poverty today in a world with such a high technical capacity to create wealth has its roots in the economic, social and political systems, all of which have failed to deliver the promised results to more than a fraction of the world's population. While some progress has been made in some countries, the numbers of poor have continued to grow, and in many countries today the situation is degrading rather than improving. For such countries, the future seems grim.

Consequences

It is difficult to predict the consequences of the selection of trends and problems described above, but for none is the prognosis very good at the moment. Even worse, these problems do not exist in isolation; there is great potential for synergies and interactions. For instance, destruction of the ozone layer would increase ultra-violet radiation at the surface and could damage vast areas of oceanic plankton, the microscopic marine plants that play an important role in absorbing carbon dioxide, the principal greenhouse gas. Ultra-violet radiation could also damage crops and reduce agricultural productivity just when the demands of a growing population may eliminate all food surpluses. The poor would suffer the most from major environmental problems like climate change or widespread toxic pollution.

Free trade can have significant environmental impacts, such as through the export of hazardous wastes to poor countries where disposal costs (and precautions) are less, or even the export of whole polluting industries to profit from lax environmental regulations. Cash crops for export to repay debt may replace local food crops, leading to nutritional deficiencies and even famine, not to mention over-stressed soils and declining productivity.

As conditions worsen in the poor over-populated countries, social, economic, environmental and often political circumstances will combine to produce swelling numbers of refugees, people leaving their homes and fleeing for their survival, or just in the hope of better opportunities than the non-existent ones at home. In the absence of new frontier areas able to absorb them, they will be crowding at the gates, and slipping under the fences, of all the wealthier countries. The logic of the pressures now building, as well as recent experience, suggest that massive movements of refugees and displaced persons will become a dominant feature of the planet's social and political landscape. The problem will be difficult to ignore, and equally difficult to respond to. There is already a growing tendency in the industrialized countries to adopt a fortress mentality, to seal the borders, keep the immigrants out, raise protectionist barriers and turn inward, but in today's world, that would be economic suicide and a political dead end. On the other hand, there are too many cases where expulsion, prison or even death are seen as the easy solutions to problems with ethnic, religious and cultural minorities. In extreme cases, government breaks down completely, allowing societies to descend into chaos and anarchy. The world has become too interdependent for withdrawal to be a reasonable option, yet it lacks sufficient cohesion and solidarity for intervention to be politically possible.

The only ultimate solution to the fundamental problem of the extremes of wealth and poverty between nations is a voluntary sharing of wealth in a effort to bring greater economic and social justice, within an international framework to ensure the equitable use of resources. The effort required can be estimated by comparison with the recent experience of Germany. There, one of the world's wealthiest countries and strongest economies is trying to bring up to its economic level the former East Germany, which shares the same language and culture, and was only distinguished by some forty years of separation and unequal development. The economic and social shock caused to Germany by this simplest of all cases highlights the kind of effort that will be required to help the masses of Asia, Africa and Latin America reach more of a planetary economic and social equilibrium.

Beyond these questions, the internal inconsistencies of the Western economic system as presently structured, the accumulation of public, corporate and personal debt in key industrialized countries, the lack of adequate regulatory mechanisms at the international level able to stabilize currencies and trade balances and to control speculation, and the persistent preference of the political leadership in most countries for self interest over the common good, do not bode well for the immediate future. The capitalist society, having crowed victory over its communist rival, may find that it is equally fragile and vulnerable to an economic decline or collapse.

Notes

1. Meadows et al. (1972).
2. Meadows et al. (1992).

CHAPTER 4

The theory of ecos

The complexity of economic and social systems and relations within and between countries makes it difficult to see the root causes of the problems that assail the world today. Yet until the causes are clearly analysed, it will be difficult to search for solutions. The systems of the natural world, both of organisms and of the communities and ecosystems they build, resemble those of human society, and are easier to analyse objectively because we can look at them from outside. It is therefore logical to seek in natural systems a theoretical framework that explains their structure and function, and that can, by analogy, shed light on human social systems as well. Such a framework can help us to observe and measure how the systems work, and ultimately to manage and develop them more effectively.

Just as mathematics clarifies many processes by symbolizing them in abstract form according to set rules and conventions, so can an abstract systems representation help us to understand the essential features of any kind of economic or ecological system and to demonstrate their underlying unity. This is the aim of the framework of characteristics and principles making up the theory of ecos, a term proposed here for generalized functional systems. The basic concept is very simple, although it may seem complex at first. Many of the ideas come from systems thinking,[1] although they are extended here. They involve an important change in perspective from that traditional in Western culture. Instead of emphasizing static entities, the focus is on dynamic systems and the processes of change. We must think in terms of verbs rather than nouns, of actions and processes rather than things. Instead of seeing everything revolving around ourselves, our culture or our country, we must recognize that there are multiple centres which must all be considered. This is the normal perspective of ecology and of many non-Western cultures.

This chapter provides a necessary foundation for applications of the theory of ecos in the chapters that follow. The abstract des-

46

cription is followed by some examples and explanations that help to put the theory into the context of the fundamental problems addressed in this book.

Definition of an eco

An *eco* (pronounced eeco, plural ecos, derived from the Greek *oikos*) is defined as *any natural or man-made functional system with internal integrity and distinct features and behaviour enclosed within clear boundaries*. This general definition will apply equally to an organism, an ecosystem, a machine, a town, a nation, the Earth, or a star. It can also be applied usefully to many human institutions.

It may help, in reading the following abstract description, to try substituting for the word eco some more familiar system such as corporation, national economy, organism, ecosystem or city. The principles apply to all of these and the analysis can be enlightening.

Any eco must have the following characteristics:

Limits: The eco must have boundaries in three dimensions that determine its form, size and limits. These boundaries may be natural or can be set arbitrarily for the purposes of analysis. They may be static or dynamic. The boundary of an animal is its skin, of a country its frontiers.

Content: The material content of the eco is its resource base or capital. For a corporation, its content is its physical assets and employees; for a farm, its land, building, implements, water supply and workforce.

Energy: For any system to function, there must be an input of energy. This can either enter the eco from outside its boundaries, or be generated within it from stored reserves or nuclear reactions. In the latter case, the production of energy results in an internal loss to the eco. Energy is also lost from the eco through entropy, radiation or other transfers beyond its boundaries. The Earth receives energy from the sun, and also from nuclear reactions deep in its rocks. It also has stored energy reserves in its fossil fuels.

Material flux: Materials may enter an eco across its boundaries, and can be quantified as inputs. These add to the resource base of the eco. Materials may also be lost across the boundaries and thus subtract from the resource base. We absorb materials with the food we eat, and take in oxygen with the air we breathe, while giving off wastes and carbon dioxide.

Dynamics: An eco exists over time and is therefore a dynamic entity or system subject to change, for which inputs and outputs per unit of time can be measured and a balance determined. If we take in more food than we can use, we gain weight. If a country cuts its forest faster than trees can grow, its forest resource base will shrink.

Information: The materials within the eco and the processes that drive the system are organized with what may be called its information content, structure and integration. This information may be latent or functional. A government has an information content that includes its organizational structure, laws and regulations, a job description plus accumulated experience for each employee, defined relationships and forms of communication between each part of the government, and many unrecorded practices and traditions.

Communications: The materials and energy crossing the boundary of an eco can also transfer or communicate information and build connections with other ecos. A cat may see or hear a movement in the grass and know that there is a mouse to stalk. A business can receive orders for its products by mail, telephone or visits by customers.

Information content

It is the information content that is the most critical characteristic of an eco, but this has not been given enough attention in systems theory. This *information on the organization and integration of the eco is the critical factor determining its value or 'wealth'*, a wealth that has been largely missed in economics. Information is the difference between a sonnet by Shakespeare and a random assortment of the same letters. In the former, the letters are codes for words with defined meanings, arranged in sentences which themselves communicate further meanings and feelings which we consider as part of our cultural wealth; in the latter, the letters carry no information. If the poem is recited, the same information is coded and communicated in the vibrations of the air that we hear as sound. The information in the sonnet is latent on the printed page, and it must be read to become functional and have an effect. Similarly, a watch has an information content reflected in its structure that defines the shape of each part and the interrelationships and connections of all the parts to produce an accurate timepiece on which we can place a value related to its function. In a watch that has stopped, the information is only stored or latent; only when the watch is running is the information useful and functional. If the watch is hit with a hammer, these interrelationships are disrupted, destroying its function and reducing its value even though the quantity of materials has not changed.

This information, in essence, has no set material existence; it is independent of either the materials or energy through which it is expressed or finds form. It is like an idea that has not yet been spoken or set down on paper. One way information is recognized economically in our society is through intellectual property rights like patents and copyrights, but otherwise we take it for granted and do not generally recognize its importance.

An eco can have other characteristics determined by its functional systems, information content, and exchanges with its surroundings, such as the ability to grow, to reproduce, and to interact with other ecos. Most organisms have these characteristics. Ecos may be nested, such that an eco can contain many subsystems which can also be defined as ecos. The limits on their functioning may be set by any of the above characteristics not controlled by the eco. A school may contain various classes, each with a number of students, who are themselves made up of many organs and billions of cells, each with a certain autonomy and defined functions.

In this abstract sense, an eco is a more-or-less arbitrarily defined spatial entity, which we can use to understand better how a particular system works or behaves. The fact that we define boundaries allows us to quantify transfers across those boundaries as distinct from the processes taking place within the boundaries. What is important about the concept is that it requires us to consider all the characteristics that are the essential properties of any eco, and which determine how it functions and therefore how it can be observed, measured and managed.

With the eco as a unifying concept, we can also redefine ecology as the study or knowledge of ecos and economics as the management of ecos. Both then take on a larger sense than in their traditional usage, and their complementarity becomes evident.

Energy flow

The second law of thermodynamics requires that any system be continually running down as energy is degraded through entropy, which is the conversion of concentrated energy into diffuse heat. The fact that so many complex systems exist demonstrates that a reverse process is also at work. *A system organized as an eco can use the energy flowing through it to build its information content.* It is this latter process that allows an eco to exist and develop. The tendency towards increasing complexity and efficiency, observable in many evolutionary processes in the natural world, is the result of this development of information content, structure and connectivity.

The ability of an eco to use its systems and the flow of energy to accumulate information and build interconnectedness is its most distinguishing characteristic. It is a law as essential to our understanding of the natural world as are the laws of physics and chemistry, since it is this characteristic that has given rise to all higher forms of existence. It could perhaps be called the law of ecodynamics. In its fundamental form it can be expressed as follows:

> Energy can drive functional systems to increase their information content and connections, either independently or through the influence of other systems, building ever more complex systems.

The concept of ecos helps us to understand this process by defining entities within which we can observe how the process works in a particular location at a particular scale. For instance, the nuclear energy released by a star can generate elements and forces that lead to the formation of a planetary system within which, under ideal circumstances like those of our own sun, life can originate and develop. Living things use the energy captured from the sun to go through many generations, gradually evolving and improving from, say, simple mosses through ferns to giant trees. We use chemical energy from the food we eat to power our sense organs and nervous system as we learn and think, acquiring knowledge. A factory uses energy to power its tools, transform its materials into products, transport its raw materials and finished goods, and thus increase its net worth. Its workers use their food energy to operate its machines, and perhaps to develop new products and processes. In all these cases, the energy is diffused and lost through entropy, but the functional process it powers improves the system.

Dynamics

Ecos are, by definition, dynamic systems, and change is therefore one of their essential characteristics. There must be movement of materials, energy and information within (or in and out of) the system. This movement can be in any direction, but that direction is important, and ultimately it must be in reasonable balance for the ecos to survive. Successful ecos tend to be self-regulating, and thus able to keep their size, structure and operational characteristics within supportable limits.

The behaviour of an eco also demonstrates several other characteristics. In a perfectly constant environment, with identical inflows and outflows, an eco will tend towards a steady state. However, this is an ideal condition and is probably never found in practice. Variability in boundary conditions and inputs will keep an eco in a constant state of change and adaptation. Success is the ability of an eco to maintain a neutral or net positive balance across its boundaries. Any specific eco will have an optimal size determined by its form, structure, and the economies or diseconomies of scale inherent in its system processes, all of which are defined by its information content. An eco that grows too fast or too large may destroy itself unless it is able to fragment or divide to reproduce itself in smaller form. A continuing negative balance in an eco will cause it to shrink, leading eventually to system failure and the disintegration of the eco. *The balance of imports to and exports from an eco is thus critical to its survival.*

The rates or speed at which various processes in an eco take place are also important. These include the rates of flows across boundaries and the rates of processes within the eco. Slow rates or time lags may allow for adjustments, where faster rates may overwhelm the system. On the other hand, a slow or inefficient eco may be at a disadvantage in its larger environment, where it may have to compete with other ecos.

Information is not tied to a particular system or collection of materials; it is lost when an eco disintegrates, but it can also be transmitted or inherited through a chain of successful ecos. *The constant turnover in materials within the system and the flow of energy towards entropy are balanced by this accumulation, transmission and perpetuation of information within ecos.* An increase in information may be reflected in an increase in efficiency or adaptability. Such information may allow the improved intake or capture of resources, their more efficient use or reduced loss, or higher states of integration, increasing the success of the eco. It is also reflected in the development of homeostatic mechanisms that allow self-regulation to ensure the balance and survival of the eco. As the information content of an eco increases, its preservation and perpetuation become increasingly important. The more highly evolved an eco, the more its management of information becomes important.

Structure

There seem to be limits to the amount of complexity and inter-connectivity possible in a system before it reaches the point of diminishing returns. One way an eco can manage such problems of the limits imposed by scale and complexity is through the subdivision of systems and tasks among different ecos that may be nested or concentric (i.e. one inside another), or spatially related, diversified and interacting. This permits both decentralization and specialization which can simplify interconnections and increase efficiency. The result is increasing diversity among ecos, in which their spatial variation, distribution and modes of interaction also become import-ant. Such relationships among ecos can range from exploitation and competition through parasitism and symbiosis to complete inter-dependence. These communities of ecos may themselves be con-sidered ecos at a higher level of complexity, created through the increasing information content of developing ecos interacting at the lower level.

While each level of organization and complexity may function and use information in quite a distinct way that is not predictable from one type of eco to another and from one level to the next, the basic principles of ecos still apply. Thus, understanding the informa-tion content and integration, its storage, transmission and use as expressed in its structure and functioning, is the key to understanding any eco at any scale of organization.

At the simplest level of minerals, information is largely embodied in the laws of physics and the atomic and chemical characteristics of matter. It is these qualities, for instance, that cause two molecules to react always in the same way under identical conditions. Living things are ecos that have developed the capacity to grow and repro-duce, which has been perpetuated by their ability to store information in concentrated form in the genetic code of DNA and to duplicate and transmit it through a continuing line of ecos (organisms). In ecosystems, the information content of the system is not held centrally but is recorded by the organisms as they have co-evolved towards increasing levels of interaction and interdependence. Human beings raise this capacity to another whole level of information, represented by abstract thought and reasoning, language, culture and science, recorded in memory and the media and transmitted through education, and we are now extending the process even further through the invention of information technologies. We have even developed the possibility of conscious control and management of the evolutionary processes of our own ecos, whether they be corporations, nations or economic systems. The ultimate eco, at least within our experience, is the whole human civilization on this planet, in which the information content has grown far beyond what any individual can assimilate or comprehend. Nonetheless, the fundamental principles of ecos continue to apply to the whole, as they do to the parts.

Functions

There are several characteristics which are common to the internal workings of ecos, regardless of their simplicity or complexity, and which can be used to describe the functioning of the system. First are the composition, structure, spatial relationships and mechanical and chemical interactions of the internal resource base, which can be described and measured. There will be some sort of transport or circulatory system to receive inputs, redistribute materials within the system, and export outputs, and these movements can be quantified. The balance in the materials accounts is critical, with the maximum and minimum determined by the size limits of the system, unless growth can be relieved by reproduction. The second characteristic is the energy pathway through the system, and the mechanisms and efficiency with which the energy is utilized. In some cases, temperature regulation within the system, and the discharge of degraded energy as waste heat can also be important. The third and most important characteristic is the storage and use of information within the system, including the signalling and control mechanisms, which may be mechanical, chemical, electrical or symbolic (i.e. language, numerical data and money). There seem to be no limits to the amount of information which a system can utilize, with increased information and integration permitting levels of complexity, size, productivity and efficiency for which no end is in sight, apart from the practical limits imposed by the planet itself. *The value of an eco is thus best measured by its information content and connections*; anything that degrades the information content reduces its value accordingly.

Efficiency

One of the basic evolutionary pressures is for efficiency, that is producing more with less. In energy terms, this means generating more work, movement or other activity for each unit of energy; in material terms, using less material at lower cost to achieve a similar or better result. Efficiency can also come from storing and using larger amounts of information, and is, in itself, an expression of that information. Increased efficiency often comes from greater strength, smaller distances, faster speeds and less expenditure of resources to maintain essential balances. These imply greater precision, more scientific knowledge applied in better use of materials and energy, and other applications of increased information content. Efficiency is one of the measures of the effective use of information in ecos.

In human ecos, efficiency can be reflected in the numbers of people that can be supported with a high quality of life, the effectiveness of communication within and between social groups, and the maintenance or increase in total information storage and use over time. In this context, an efficient, successful or more highly evolved eco is one that at least maintains itself, if not advancing or reproducing, and that performs its functions, including supporting other ecos dependent on it, for the least through-put of energy and materials, generally involving the maximum use of information. At higher levels of organization, efficiency may be reflected in the productivity or density of ecos supported, and the stability and durability of the whole system.

While the tendency to increase complexity and efficiency over time seems to be a natural characteristic of ecos, it results from a set of conflicting processes. In a constant environment, the most efficient ecos present will come to dominate, specializing for maximum efficiency in that particular set of conditions and monopolizing resources. This could slow or block further evolution. Also, specialization increases vulnerability, and increased size creates inertia. Variability in the environment can alternately favour ecos with different characteristics, or perhaps smaller and more flexible ones, increasing diversity. However, extreme variability tends to select for a few resistant ecos that can adapt to a wide range of conditions but are less efficient in any of them. The pressures from interactions with other ecos can also increase the evolutionary pressure on ecos, selecting those with certain characteristics and eliminating others. The balance between these different processes determines the final result. The length of time they have been operating is also important, since the process of perfecting an eco is a slow one, and seldom goes to completion before conditions change.

Examples

A simple example can illustrate how the general theory can be applied in practice. Take, for instance, the motor of an automobile. The boundaries of this eco are the outer form of the motor. Its resource base is the metal and other materials of which the motor is made. The input of energy is transported in chemical form in the fuel that powers its operation. Energy is transferred out of the eco as mechanical force to drive the car, and is also lost as waste heat by radiation and through the hot exhaust. The inputs are the fuel and the air taken in for combustion, plus occasional additions of lubricating oil and coolant. These are balanced through the equal loss of exhaust gases containing combustion products, and the draining of lubricant and coolant. The wear of engine parts also results in some loss of materials which may ultimately threaten the continued functioning of the motor. The most critical feature of the motor is its engineering design (information content), which determines with great precision the content, shape and interrelationships of all the parts, and the efficiency with which it converts energy into mechanical power. Information transferred to the motor through the throttle determines its speed and the rate of transfer of materials and energy across its boundaries. Wear, being a loss of materials and precision, is thus also a loss of information content; if it proceeds beyond a certain point or a part breaks, the information content is degraded too far for the motor to work properly and it stops. A motor is a simple eco that cannot repair or reproduce itself, but must be created and maintained through outside inputs. As an eco, it can be characterized functionally by its fuel consumption, efficiency, power output, etc., all of which can be determined by measuring the transfers across its boundaries.

A house could be another example of an eco. It is created as a bounded entity by the assembly of materials during its construction, using the information of the architect's plan and the builders' skills, in order to perform a certain function. It receives energy inputs of electricity and perhaps heating or cooking fuel, and loses energy as light and waste heat. The people living in it may add to and subtract from its material contents and information content at will, possibly changing its form and function. If it catches fire, most of its material and information content will be lost, and it will cease to exist as a functional entity.

Ecos as systems

The theory of ecos is an extension of systems theory as it has been developed over several decades. Others have also used this approach to understand the workings of natural and human systems.[2] What is added here is the emphasis on information storage and flow as the key factor in understanding system functioning, and the evolutionary drive to use energy flow in the system to increase information content, structure and efficiency. It is this information dimension that helps to bridge our understanding of natural and human social ecos, as well as to incorporate the more abstract cultural, moral and spiritual dimensions of human systems into the theoretical framework.

The linking of a systems approach with the evolutionary analyses of biology and ecology adds a temporal perspective that helps to clarify our own situation. We tend to be so short-sighted and concerned with our own immediate problems that we fail to see where we have come from and where we are going. The concept of an eco as a functional system responsible for processes *over time* takes on a special importance. Just as trying to stay balanced on a stationary bicycle is very different from riding one, so is the dynamic dimension essential to our understanding of any eco or other functional system. There are, of course, many dimensions of time, from the nanoseconds important to the latest computer circuits, the time to the next meal for a starving refugee, or a human lifetime, to the aeons of biological evolution and cosmic processes. Each scale of time has its importance, just as each scale in space has appropriate ecos. Dynamic systems can operate at all scales.

The evolution of information capacity

The vast sweep of evolving systems and the ways they incorporate information are clarified by the concept of ecos. Each level of system organization has followed certain, often distinct, rules, laws or principles which embody the information determining how the elements of the system relate to each other and interact in an integrated way.

The first level of ecos, which we are now beginning to understand through research in high-energy physics, concerns the nature and behaviour of sub-atomic particles and the relations between matter and energy. We try to explain the information governing their interactions through the rules and formulas of quantum physics. As matter became organized into atoms through the application of these rules, a new set of inherent principles came into application, governing the interactions between atoms. We call the body of information for this level of organization chemistry. The most complex forms of atomic matter in space condensed out into planets like the Earth, where molecules of increasing complexity could accumulate and interact, finally achieving the ability to reproduce themselves through enzymatic processes, passing the information determining their chemical structure on to other molecules.

The next great breakthrough was the evolution of molecules such as the DNA in genes and chromosomes capable of storing and transmitting information for the whole set of enzymes and other molecules in a functioning and reproducing chemical system, creating what we call life. Our knowledge of this level of organization is collected in the science of biology. Living biological systems were made possible by a new level of information storage and communication that permitted higher levels of integration according to new principles and rules, such as those being explored in genetics. The next leap forward was in the evolution of nervous systems capable of collecting and storing information sensed or experienced by the organism, making learning possible. However, this learned information was lost with the death of the organism, and each new generation had to acquire it again, through trial and error, where it was not coded genetically as instincts.

Ultimately, the more highly evolved animals, with elaborate sense perception and the rudiments of communication, developed the ability to learn from each other by observation and imitation. This made it possible to transmit some learned information from generation to generation outside of that preserved in genetic material. Such information transmission, the beginning of education, permitted higher levels of social organization. The evolution of the human brain, with its capacities for extended memory storage and for abstract and symbolic reasoning, led to the development of language through which the collective memory of a people, as well as a certain level of hunting, agricultural and material technology, could be passed on through descriptions, oral tradition and legend. At this time, civilization was limited by the collective memory capacity of the community and the ability to transmit that stored information directly from person to person.

The invention of writing and, ultimately, of printing extended information storage beyond the capacity of human memory and improved its accuracy and the geographic range of its transmission. For some centuries, books and documents could travel no faster than people, transported by sailing ships at sea or by animals on land, slowing the rate of information transmission and limiting the size of effective social ecos. It was within this environment that the nation states were first formed.

This information barrier was broken in 1844 when the invention of the telegraph began the electrical communication of information. This technological revolution in information storage and transmission is still continuing through the rapid multiplication of electronic media. It will permit the creation of ever more highly developed and integrated civilizations. In particular, the near instantaneous exchange of masses of information around the planet makes a true world human eco possible. The implications of this recent transformation of our human environment on the operation of all ecos, including our own, will be explored in the chapters that follow.

Without this evolutionary perspective of progression in ecos, it is easy to be left with a profound sense of depression when reviewing the present social, economic, environmental and political problems described in Chapters 2 and 3. Our multiple crises make it difficult to imagine how the world will pull out of what seems like a nose-dive to destruction. Yet there is an amazing resilience in both natural and human systems. There have been catastrophes before; civilizations have fallen and others have risen from the ashes. While the transition from our present excesses will inevitably be difficult, we can be confident that this is only a transition. Many of the trials and tribulations of today are in fact the growing pains associated with the difficult social transition from the relatively isolated, sovereign and independent ecos of our nation states to a new level of global integration within the eco of what is becoming, under the impulse of technology and changing values, an interdependent world society.

Why a theory of ecos?

The theory of ecos provides a framework which demonstrates the complementarity of the natural, economic and human systems. The natural world is full of ecos of various scales and dimensions – cells, organisms, ecosystems, the planet itself – in which the information content has accumulated in functional systems over billions of years by the operation of natural laws. Some examples are given in the next chapter. These ecos have become the primary resources for our material civilization, which we now use and abuse at our will. Our own human ecos evolved largely unconsciously until humans began to try to steer their course and manage their variations through such means as economic theory and practice. The application of the theory of ecos to economics shows its weakness as a management tool because of its failure to incorporate many externalities, and in particular to account for the importance of information and connectivity within all systems, as discussed in Chapter 6. An analysis using ecos can also clarify our own nature as human beings and the complexities of human communities, as reviewed in Chapters 7 and 8. It can suggest ways to guide our own social evolution in more satisfactory directions.

The integration of all these elements is necessary to define the principal parameters of the modern global human eco, parameters which must all be in balance if the eco is to survive. We are now in a situation where information flows around the world so well that we are fully conscious of our plight, even if many dimensions of it are not fully understood or appreciated. We can see the gross inequalities between countries and peoples, the injustice caused by prejudice, intolerance, power struggles and ethnic cleansing. We have thus, for the first time in human history, reached the brink of social maturity, when we can acquire the knowledge and capacity to guide and manage our own future economic, social and cultural evolution. In fact, we have unwittingly so interfered with the natural systems of this planet that we shall probably be obliged to manage these as well if the equilibria and life-support systems so necessary for our own survival are to be maintained. In exercising our responsibility for management, we must be able to integrate and interrelate all parts of the system. Our present problems are largely the result of the narrow partial approaches to management represented by present-day economics. We must therefore begin to redesign, renew and integrate the information and institutional systems necessary for the management of the enormously complex eco we call human civilization.

The theory of ecos has important implications for the way we view human institutions and social structures. It suggests that the best measure of the efficiency and success of such structures is in their content, flow and use of information. The greater the number of contacts and interconnections between people, the better information can flow between them and the more use can be made of it, with the whole process adding to the store or capital of information in the ecos. This means that processes of consultation, group decision-making and teamwork should be more creative and efficient than vertical structures of line management, or dispersed relations where each person or other functional unit works more or less in isolation, without relations with other people or ecos.

The analysis of various ecos also shows that there are optimum levels of information flow and connectivity. Too much can saturate a system and be as inefficient as too little. This is where decentralization, individual autonomy and flexibility become important. They allow the subdivision of complex ecos into smaller units and nested sub-units to maintain maximum internal cohesion while permitting optimal connections with other parts of the larger systems. The more complex a system becomes, the more important becomes this balance between connectivity and independence, central coordination and decentralized action, in the interest of making best use of the available capital and information and of adding a new wealth of information to it. This is the way to achieve unity in diversity.

Thus, human systems that tend to limit or control information flow and to concentrate power are counter-productive, as are those in which communications and coordination break down and anarchy results. This provides a basis for testing existing institutions in our society, evaluating their weaknesses and failings, and identifying the solutions needed to remedy their deficiencies. We need ways to measure and monitor the information content, flow and connectivity within human systems, perhaps producing some kind of index of integration, and pinpointing areas where barriers have been raised and communications have broken down.

There are implications of this type of structuring for the values and behaviour of the individual person as well. Openness to others, freedom from prejudice, a desire to serve others, and a willingness to communicate and exchange, would favour participation in the system, whereas selfishness, fear, defensiveness and withdrawal, or pride and a desire for power, control and domination, would be undesirable and damaging to the system. These themes will be developed in the chapters that follow.

Notes

1. Similar approaches using systems analysis techniques can be found in Koestler (1967), Capra (1981), Henderson (1988), among others.
2. Koestler (1967), Capra (1981), Henderson (1988).

CHAPTER 5

Ecos in nature

The natural world contains many examples of ecos that have been studied in detail, and can be used to demonstrate applications of the theory of ecos and some of its characteristics of particular interest. These characteristics reappear in other ecos, including human communities and institutions.

Microbes and plants

A bacterium is a very simple living organism, bounded by a membrane and containing a complex chemical mixture organized to maintain its life processes. Its information content resides partly in its molecular constituents, particularly enzymes, and is also coded in its genetic material (DNA). The bacterium grows by absorbing energy- and material-containing chemicals from its surroundings, often by secreting enzymes to decompose external materials into useful substances. It uses some of the chemical energy for its own metabolism and growth, releasing waste products. When it reaches a certain size, it replicates its information store of DNA and divides into two cells. If the cell grew too large without dividing, materials would not diffuse rapidly enough into and within the cell, more remote areas might lack energy or accumulate waste products, the internal chemical organization would start to break down, and the cell would die. *The size of an eco is determined by the ability of its information content to organize it and to maintain control.* This in turn depends on the sophistication of its structure, communications and transport systems. The information in the DNA controls all the processes in the cell and defines the composition of all the molecules manufactured, but it is not sufficient by itself to create a bacterium, because it requires the pre-existing chemical machinery in the cell, powered by energy, to transcribe the information coded in its structure into useful forms. Therefore every bacterial eco (cell) is derived from a previous eco.

A virus should probably not be considered an eco because it is not a complete functional system, but only a package of genetic material (information) enclosed in a protein coat that allows it to penetrate into a cell where it parasitizes the cell machinery to make its information functional and replicate itself.

A simple algal (plant) cell illustrates another level of complexity in ecos. As in most plants, the energy input is provided by sunlight, which the cell machinery captures and converts to chemical energy. This energy is stored by combining hydrogen from water and carbon from carbon dioxide into hydrocarbon molecules, absorbing the raw materials from the environment and excreting oxygen as a waste product. The machinery for this process of photosynthesis is in a sack-like structure called a chloroplast. The cells also have similar structures called mitochondria which take in oxygen to oxidize molecules with stored chemical energy, releasing the energy to drive cell processes, as well as carbon dioxide as a waste product, in the process of respiration. Both structures are discrete membrane-bounded entities which could also be considered as ecos. In fact, chloroplasts and mitochondria have their own genetic material and reproduce themselves within the cell. It is probable that they were originally derived from bacteria that learned to live within and, ultimately, became totally interdependent with an ancestral host cell. This *nesting of ecos within ecos is one way that complex systems can be kept decentralized and manageable.*

An interesting example of the steps taken by living organisms towards organizational complexity is given by the cellular slime moulds. These are single-celled amoeba-like creatures that creep around engulfing organic material as food. However, when conditions are right for reproduction, one cell will start releasing a chemical attractant that causes the cells to aggregate into a slug-like form which glides along like a multicellular organism until it finds an appropriate site. Some cells then attach themselves to the substrate, others build themselves into a rigid vertical column, and the remainder crawl up the column to the top, where they form a fruiting body and turn into spores. The dry spores are blown away and settle, and when conditions are right, they turn again into single-celled amoebae, to grow and divide and start the process over again. In this case of an eco formed by an assembly of ecos, information communicated within the massed cells causes some to sacrifice themselves in building the supporting structure so that others can propagate the species. *Specialization is another way to increase complexity, performance and efficiency,* and *individual altruism can lead to collective success.*

Some of the essential principles of biological organization can be illustrated by some simple seaweeds which grow into different forms depending on their environment. The growing cells of the plant body need only to know their orientation in the plant and their length and width in order to know which way to divide. Their pattern of divisions determines the length and width of the plant. The resulting basic fan-shaped plant form interacts with the environment. In deeper water where light is limited, the plant grows into wide flat blades, while waves and sand may damage some growing cells in shallow areas to produce dense bunches of narrow blades where protection from waves and exposure is more important. The variety of shapes and sizes of plants found in nature does not result from complicated genetic plans, but from the operation of simple developmental rules requiring few information inputs, interacting with other determining factors in the environment.[1] Thus, even a rather complex-looking and adaptable eco may in fact require only a minimum of information in a few simple organizational rules, plus some outside inputs, to guide its functional system. *Understanding the rules and the types and sources of information is the key to understanding the whole functional system.* It is the operation of the rules which allows such a self-managing system to adapt and evolve in a variety of situations.

Animals

An animal body represents an eco with a much higher development of multi-level organization and specialization. While basic physiological processes are still decentralized to the cellular level, the cells make up tissues which are combined into organs as parts of complex and highly integrated structural, digestive, circulatory, motor and nervous systems. These communicate with each other through elaborate electrical (nervous) and chemical (hormonal) control systems, showing *ever-increasing information content at higher levels of complexity.* The function of each component could be analysed as an eco in the process of determining the overall system structure and operation. However, a knowledge of the overall systems controls at the highest levels of organization of the largest eco would be necessary to understand the system, and these can have characteristics quite independent of those at the levels beneath them.

An eco can have an important *dimension of change over time.* This can be an *evolutionary* dimension over long time scales, such as the evolution of reptiles up through the dinosaurs and on to today's snakes and lizards, representing a long branching chain of ecos through many generations. Some reach a dead end and die out, while others continue to change and adapt, surviving over very long time periods. Change over time can also be *developmental*, as in the maturation of a fertilized mammalian egg through embryonic stages and juvenile forms up to adulthood. While much of the information directing an organism's development is contained in its genetic instructions, there can be a significant environmental input or inter-action, and in higher organisms some transmission of information through learning by mimicry of adults or by conscious education.

There are, in nature, examples of almost all stages in the develop-ment of ecos at different levels of organization. Social insects such as bees illustrate a community of one species of organism that can be considered an eco. Different members of the community are specialized for different functions, with the queen responsible for reproduction, the drones for mating, and the workers for constructing the hive, defence and supplying food for the whole community. Here the *social organization of the community has its own information content and means of communication*, such as the dance with which a worker that has found a new source of nectar signals to its fellow workers the direction and distance to fly in order to find it. In ants, chemical signalling is an important part of the information exchange that maintains social organization.

Ecosystems

At the higher levels of the natural organization of ecos stand complex ecosystems such as tropical forests and coral reefs, which have some of the greatest levels of productivity and complexity (thousands of species on a single reef or in a single tree) recorded on the planet. Coral reefs are among the most ancient of surviving ecosystems, with some species little changed over millions of years. They occur in the relatively constant environment of tropical seas, and have thus had both the time and the conditions necessary to evolve extremely high levels of information content, integration and efficiency. Their high productivity is maintained in spite of what is often a resource-poor environment. Tropical waters are so clear and beautiful because they are largely devoid of plankton and nutrients. Coral reef ecosystems are very efficient at trapping what resources are available, recycling scarce materials within the system, intercepting the maximum amount of solar energy on their elaborate and multi-layered reef surfaces, and transferring energy very effectively within the system. Reefs maintain information not only in their great genetic diversity, but in the high levels of relationships between different species, symbionts and other ecos. The overall balance of the system is, in fact, maintained by a highly dynamic interplay of many species at smaller spatial scales.

The theory of ecos can provide a framework for an analysis of the basic workings of a coral reef ecosystem, although the detail cannot be reviewed here. An early attempt at a systems analysis of a coral reef ecosystem identified 104 compartments or subsystems, all interacting, whose contents and relationships would need to be analysed and quantified to get some generalized sense of how the system worked.[2] With thousands of species, each containing many ecos and making up many others at multiple levels of interaction, the complexity is mind-boggling. What is important to understand here is that the ecosystem is *integrated and connected through many different systems of exchange and control that maintain the balance of the system and convey much of its information content.*

For instance, the flow of materials through the coral reef ecosystem can be understood in terms of carbon, nitrogen, phosphorus and various micro-nutrients. Since the reef is bathed in seawater, water and oxygen are omnipresent and not normally of any special concern. The supply of carbon is usually not a problem since it comes from the atmosphere as dissolved carbon dioxide. Carbon is important not only for its role as the atomic backbone of all organic materials from which living things are built, but also because many reef organisms precipitate carbon in calcium carbonate, the lime from which many shells and skeletons are built and which accumulates to make the reef framework. The carbon cycle of the reef is thus critical to its operation and very existence, and measuring the flow and use of carbon tells much about its success, much as measuring flows of money describes important characteristics of an economy. Fixed nitrogen and phosphorus are both critical to life, and can be in very short supply in tropical seawater. The ability of corals and other organisms to capture whatever drifting plankton and other sea life may come their way gives the reef a small supply of these materials which is then recycled very efficiently within the reef system. A few reef organisms can also fix atmospheric nitrogen, increasing the available supply. Since the currents flowing over a reef will always carry away some materials, it is essential that this loss be made up through the capture or manufacture of replacements. Phosphorus is often one of the most limiting materials for the reef in this respect.

The capture and use of energy by the reef is another critical feature. The reef system generates very large surface areas covered with plants and animals containing the photosynthetic machinery necessary to trap solar energy and store it in organic molecules. The reef is thus able to capture a significant part of the available renewable energy from sunlight. It may seem surprising that animals can do this, but many reef animals, including corals and giant clams, have tiny symbiotic plants living inside them. The plants provide the host animals with food in exchange for lodging and fertilization with the animals' waste products. The animals themselves thus become almost like a closed system, making for high efficiency. Many other grazers, filter-feeders and scavengers pick up any available energy-carrying materials, so that little is lost or wasted. This is why the reef can support such a high density of living organisms despite its very poor environment.

The key to the system that makes this efficiency possible is its high information content and interconnection, reflected in the many and complex ways the reef organisms work together in structured and specialized relationships. The rules for these interactions have become programmed through evolution into the genetic codes of reef plants and animals. For instance, a small species of fish and a shrimp normally share a burrow in the sand; the shrimp digs the burrow and the fish, which has better eyes, stands watch and warns the shrimp when both should hide from danger in the burrow. Cleaner fish keep highly visible stations, advertising their services, and large predatory fish come not to eat them but to have the parasites picked off, even from inside their mouth. Information is exchanged through visual signals and patterns, chemical signals, sounds and vibrations, and direct contact, and probably through other means yet to be discovered. Reef organisms also make use of outside information – daily cycles of light and darkness, the phases of the moon, subtle seasonal changes, weather patterns – all of which help to signal and synchronize various processes and forms of behaviour on the reef. It is the complexity of these relationships that has allowed so many kinds of organisms to find a place and a function in the reef system, and this in turn has brought the productivity and efficiency of the reef as an integrated system to a very high level of dynamic perfection.

Often when people interfere with a natural system such as a coral reef, it is the *information content of the system that is degraded first*, as pollution interferes with delicately balanced reef processes or communications mechanisms, or the selective removal of certain species by heavy fishing upsets relationships and breaks links in the system. Imagine what would happen in a city if all the bakers were poisoned and all the police were removed from the community.

To understand how a coral reef system works as a model eco, one might start with a study of the flow of carbon in the system, since carbon is critical to the capture and release of energy, to the transfer of materials, and to the construction of the reef framework. Yet even detailed studies of carbon stocks and flows would be insufficient to describe or manage the system. Much of the information content would be missed. An imbalance caused by excess nitrogen or phosphorus could completely upset the system without the cause ever being apparent in the carbon cycle. The removal of many fish by humans or passing predators would show as a certain loss of fixed carbon without any indication as to the cause.

Exactly the same situation applies when money stocks and flows are measured to understand and manage an economy. Figures for capital investments, savings, monetary flows, money supply, etc., are useful but are far from adequate to describe the system, as the theory of ecos demonstrates. Economic management based on such monetary measures often fails because many other important flows, and much of the information content and connectivity, which help to determine the behaviour of the system, are missed. This theme is developed in the next chapter.

Notes

1. These ideas were developed in my doctoral research in the late 1960s, and for the more technically minded can be found in Dahl (1971).

2. The application of systems analysis to the coral reef ecosystem was developed by a team of eighty specialists in the early 1970s, but the conceptual work could not be followed up for lack of funding and inadequate computer power at the time. A summary was published in Dahl et al. (1974).

CHAPTER 6

A more organic economics

There has been extensive work over the past few decades exploring the weaknesses in the present approaches to economics and proposing alternative systems, including some that tries to bridge economics and the environment. The ideas of E.F. Schumacher and his *Small is Beautiful*[1] helped to inspire a movement centred in Britain around Ekins, Robertson, etc., to develop a new economics.[2] In America, similar critiques have been developed by Henderson, Daly, Costanza, and others,[3] but they have tended to stay very much in the American context. Daly and Cobb even advocate an isolationist retreat from engagement with the rest of the world because of the enormity of the problems the US faces and the impossibility of bringing real change elsewhere.[4] If this work shares a common weakness, it is that of being heavily anchored in Western society and thus insufficiently universal in perspective. This may be inevitable, since it is Western economics that has caused or contributed to many world problems. It is not possible in this short study to review all of this other work or to integrate it fully, but many of the economic ideas touched on here find their echo and elaboration in the work of the authors cited and their colleagues. Interested readers are encouraged to explore them further.

Economics has traditionally dealt with the measurement and management of productivity and exchanges in human communities, just as ecology has focused on understanding productivity and exchanges in natural communities. Their convergence is only recent, since the need for management was the driving force in studying human systems of exchange, while in natural systems, their scientific study long preceded any need to manage them. Furthermore, there are additional levels of complexity and a much higher level of information content in human society. Yet just as the theory of ecos can help to clarify the workings of complex natural systems, so can it throw light on the strengths and weaknesses of present economic systems and suggest improvements.

Organic economics

It may help in considering the renewal of economics to explore some basic economic concepts and mechanisms from the perspective of equivalent biological systems. Growth, for instance, is almost universal in biology, but always within limits. Any biological system, such as a microbial community that grows explosively, will quickly overshoot the capacity of its environment, and either exhaust some factor such as oxygen or food necessary to sustain life, or be killed off by its own accumulated waste products, and thus will collapse. An organism generally grows until it reaches a mature size for its species, at which point growth slows or stops, or the organism divides or reproduces so that growth can begin again. Most growth, in fact, is really compensation for the inevitable depreciation that affects all physical objects. Growth in nature is largely replacement or renewal. Leaves grow in the spring to replace those that fell in the autumn; young grow to replace their elders that have died or been eaten. The concept of endless or unlimited growth so dear to economics is a biological impossibility and an economic fantasy. Living off growth is like trying to live by creaming off productivity during a young organism's spurt of growth toward maturity; in nature this would stunt the organism. If a juvenile technology can be compared to a juvenile organism, then an attempt by investors to draw excessive dividends from a growing technology during this critical development phase could be short-lived and economically damaging.

Interest is a related concept which, if compounded as is customary in economic calculations, produces endless growth that either reaches an unsustainable limit, or must be compensated in a hidden fashion by inflation (the erosion of the value on which the interest is calculated). The biological equivalent is the excess of productivity over consumption, which is generally zero or a tiny fraction in balanced biological systems (the only kind that survive for any length of time). This implies that only very low rates of real interest are healthy and sustainable in economics, and any attempt to increase the rate of return unduly will ultimately lead to instability and collapse. The traditional prohibitions on usury in some cultures may be an ancient acknowledgement of this situation.

Both of these factors suggest that the current mania of institutional investors to chase the highest possible returns around the world produces only short-term gains for the lucky or skilful, but at a considerable long-term cost to other economic actors. The requirement for balance in healthy ecos would suggest that capital investors should be satisfied with a limited but steady return as a sign of economic success. The real growth in wealth of human ecos should be in the intangible but unlimited information components, including knowledge and culture.

There is even an organic equivalent of market mechanisms in such things as the behaviour of organisms in an ecosystem. Each organism is an independent actor trying to maximize its own benefit, which basically means surviving to reproduce and perpetuate its own genes. It thus competes for resources both with others of its own species and with other species in the community. The division of resources is based on supply and demand. A predator, for instance, may maximize its own benefit by picking the prey that represent the best quality food that it can catch for the least effort (or cost). As certain prey become scarce, their relative 'cost' rises so that others may become more attractive. Human markets perhaps mimic this example too closely, with an 'eat or be eaten' mentality rather than a search for mutual benefit. What is different about natural organic 'markets' is that they involve only immediate transactions and are not subject to speculation or manipulation. Access to information is roughly the same for all organisms based on what they can sense in their immediate surroundings, and a balance is generally quite easily struck. An over-exploited organism becomes scarce (expensive to find), and the pressures move elsewhere to more accessible resources. The additional human capacity of abstract reasoning, which leads us to anticipate the future and to want to modify or conceal market information, requires compensating controls to allow the market mechanism to function with maximum efficiency in the interest of all participants.

Even if economic markets are simply seen as impersonal mechanisms to distribute goods and services most efficiently, they have proven very difficult to manage in practice for this end. However, such a mechanistic view of economic operations will not meet the needs of a human society in which efficiency needs to be balanced with other necessary characteristics of ecos, which can be expressed in human terms by the ideals of unity and justice.[5] The higher levels of social organization in human communities make possible and even require a shift from self-centred to more altruistic forms of behaviour. This will require new economic models to implement and reflect the even higher levels of efficiency possible in more highly integrated systems.

Economic ecos

To understand these new perspectives, it may help to trace briefly the historical development of economic entities. The first economic and social eco was the family, living together and looking after its own needs. As humans moved beyond the stage of complete self-sufficiency in the family unit, the first exchanges, beyond the strong simply taking what they wanted from the weak, were by barter, where each had something the other wanted and these were therefore traded. Barter quickly proved to be inflexible as more items were exchanged and additional parties became involved. A trader might have to take something he did not want, in order to exchange it later for something he needed. Soon compact but valuable metals like gold, silver and bronze took on this intermediate role, and money was created as an intermediate value and a symbolic representation of goods and services being exchanged. This gave the currency an information content or meaning beyond its intrinsic value, represented by the prices in precious metals for the different things being exchanged. It allowed for the accounting of different things in a common numerical measure, giving such numbers a particular value in society. Money therefore became the language for the information content of economic ecos.

The market system of today is just an elaboration on this basic trading function. The price or value of each good or service is set, in principle, by the law of supply and demand, with money serving as the intermediate denomination permitting great flexibility in exchanges. People sell their labour for a money wage which allows them to purchase everything they need and/or can afford. The system of market ecos has become highly developed, with different national currencies, management of the money supply and interest rates, booms and recessions, and teams of government economists adjusting the economic levers while businesses, investors and speculators are all out trying to maximize their own advantage. In terms of the theory of ecos, the intelligence and enterprise of the many in a theoretical free market have a higher information content and more potential connections than the few trying to run a centrally planned economy. This should result in greater efficiency and flexibility if the trend is in fact towards integration rather than anarchy.

The role of money in highly developed economies has extended beyond the simple information function as a common denomination to interrelate the goods and services being exchanged. Money in mass becomes a kind of liquid capital that can be invested not only in instruments of production which will generate revenue to repay the investment with interest, but also as interest-bearing loans for many non-productive purposes (current expenditure, consumption) which may cycle down through a chain of loans resulting in money earning money to expand the money supply, while debts accumulate and the money loses value through inflation. In this way money takes on a life of its own that is far removed from the real productive wealth it was supposed to measure, and this is in fact harmful to its function as a standard medium of exchange. It is amassed and manipulated in ways damaging to real economic production. Money thus becomes an abstract tool for power, domination and profit, making the rich richer without contributing to real productive activity. It may be worth asking if the amassing of such artificial wealth is not inherently destabilizing to the economy. Money may be useful in moderation, but should perhaps not be accumulated to excess in balanced, well-functioning ecos. This would justify graduated income taxes and other legal measures to prevent the acquisition of large fortunes. This issue needs to be explored further in various economic contexts.

The information content of money as a symbol for wealth depends on the complete substitutability of one good or service for another. Unfortunately, this fundamental assumption of economics does not always hold true, which is why there are so many externalities. It is a common failing in economics that widely accepted economic abstractions do not in fact correspond to concrete realities.[6] The function of money as a medium of exchange is more limited than economists would like to believe. It is not possible for a person to substitute more water for an inadequate supply of air to breathe; the result is drowning. If there is no food, you cannot eat money. The attempt to convert everything into monetary terms is thus doomed to failure. It is this insistence on money as the essential medium for defining and valuing human needs and services and the *sine qua non* of all exchanges that results in people starving because they cannot afford to buy the food available. Other approaches are needed to deal with this problem, and will be discussed below.

A more complete application of the theory of ecos to a typical economic system can demonstrate where present economic management overlooks essential controlling factors. Any economic system or eco has geographic limits, usually today a nation state within set national boundaries across which customs and tariff barriers apply, with a national currency, central bank with exchange reserves, stock and commodities markets, and other instruments of monetary and economic exchange and regulation. Within this eco there is a resource base including all the land and natural resources of the country, its property, developed resources, urban and industrial infrastructure, its workforce and human resources, its fiscal resources and everything else that can be considered as capital. The energy to power the economy comes from the primary productivity harvested in agriculture, forestry and fisheries, from fossil fuels (whether produced domestically or imported), and from some mix of other sources such as hydroelectricity, nuclear power, geothermal, wind and direct solar energy capture, etc. Some energy may be incorporated in exports, but much is used and dispersed for domestic purposes, whether to meet human needs for food, light, heat, etc., or to contribute added value in economic activities. In modern economies, there are many imports and exports, with the balance of primary commodities and finished goods imported and exported depending on how underdeveloped or industrialized the country is. The relation of these material flows to the stability of, or change in, the resource base is complex but may be significant. No country has yet prepared complete accounts of the status of its resource base, although some are now trying to develop ways of doing this through natural resources accounting. At present, development generally proceeds without attention to its long-term consequences for resources. Similarly, trade balances of imports and exports are measured financially, but not in terms of the significance of these material flows for the balance of resources, or for such environmental problems as the accumulation of wastes.

As in any eco, the most important characteristic is the information content and connectivity, including the way the system is organized to maintain itself and to provide goods and services. An empty country, with a dispersed population and rich primary resources such as oil, providing a high GNP, has a much lower information or knowledge content and level of integration than a densely populated and highly organized but largely subsistence society, where the GNP may be much lower but social and cultural richness much higher.

Information as wealth

It is here that our economic systems can be judged and found wanting, because they are founded on a very narrow view of value seen largely in terms of the financial value of material goods and productivity. The theory of ecos shows that the true value and richness of a system are not in its material content but in its information content, particularly the knowledge and experience of human beings, and in the use of that information to build inter-connections in organized communities or in productive entities such as businesses. Materials can easily be substituted or replaced. At a distance, costume jewellery is indistinguishable from the real thing. Impressions can be just as valuable as reality, and much more cost effective. However, our present economic systems are very imperfect when it comes to placing a value on information content. Such judgements often have to be made outside of economic considera-tions, and sometimes even contrary to economic logic. The decision of the US government to continue manufacturing unneeded weapons at great expense in order to keep intact the skilled labour and industrial capacity necessary to make them is a case in point. The information content of those highly specialized industries and the practical knowledge of their workforces would have been lost if they were closed, as required by market forces, and would have been extremely difficult, slow and costly to recreate if required for a future emergency. Economically, the capacity to produce a product already in surplus, for which the market is saturated, has no value. Yet if that product is indispensable, and might at some future time become scarce, the capacity to produce or maintain it may suddenly have a very high value. Our economic system cannot cope with such aspects, as indicated also by its inability to value the life-support systems of the planet. The same is true of its valuing of the information content of human beings.

The information content in an eco such as a national economy or society comes in many forms. There is first the information in its natural systems and genetic resources, the forests and grasslands, lakes and rivers, mountains, deserts and coastal waters, species and ecosystems that make up its natural heritage. This information has accumulated over millennia of evolution without any human involvement. It maintains the operation of natural systems but is there for us to use (and misuse). Then there are the systems of human exploitation of natural resources, agricultural techniques and domesticated genetic resources, adapted from long experience to each set of local conditions. Each industry has is own structure and information content, like an eco within an eco, including its processes and technologies, patents and management systems, distribution and sales networks, etc. There are transportation, communications and energy systems and a wide range of service sectors, each with its knowledge base. The intellectual structure of the society also must be included, covering scientific knowledge and research, technology, culture, educational systems, libraries and other information depositories. These are directed and balanced by systems of government, law and management. All of this is created, maintained and transmitted by people, who, apart from the natural systems, are the origin and users of all this information. This is the true wealth of a human civilization or other eco, defined much more broadly than by present economic measures.

Many of the elements of these complex systems are not bought and sold, and are thus not valued in monetary terms in the market economy. They therefore escape from present measures of wealth. They also cannot be subjected to the basic premise of a monetized system that everything is interchangeable through a monetary intermediary. A monetary system of valuation must be supplemented by other methods of valuation and distribution of resources to ensure human welfare. Measures of the various kinds of information content and services performed would be more universal as estimates of wealth than purely financial values.

To take one example of cultural information as wealth, consider a much-loved piece of classical music. Does it have a value, and if so, how much is it worth? Economists might use the measure of willingness to pay, that is how much people are prepared to pay to listen to a concert performance or to purchase a recording of the piece. But this still leaves aside the pleasure of those who may love the music but cannot afford concert tickets or recordings. Also, can one piece of music be freely substituted for another? Most people would say that the cultural heritage would be impoverished if the piece of music were lost, but that loss, while real in a social, psychological or spiritual sense, cannot easily be expressed in money. Similarly, suppose a wealthy but unbalanced person bought great works of art in order to destroy them. How could society measure the very real loss from the disappearance of a priceless cultural object?

A code of laws is another kind of information of great value to society. Generally it has been elaborated and refined over generations to define the way the community works. Laws will have been drafted, modified, perfected and codified. Judicial interpretations may have clarified many ambiguities. Institutions will have developed to give the law form, to apply it and to sanction those who fail to respect it. It is the constitution and other laws that establish institutions of government and their responsibilities. It is laws that define and set the limits on human relationships, ranging from marriage to business liability. They create tax systems to finance the operation of community institutions. They are the principal instruments for structuring human ecos. Without laws, written or unwritten, a society would collapse. But can the value of such a legal system be determined by economics? One could perhaps calculate the number of person-hours that went into developing the system, and the cost to society if it stopped functioning, but these would not be complete measures of its importance. Someone is always ready to estimate how much a new law, say on pollution control, will cost industry, but such figures are always incomplete and generally one-sided. Yet a country with an extensive and functional legal system will consider itself more developed and better off than one with many legal lacunae.

All these forms of wealth are critical components of complex human social and economic ecos. The long-term success of society depends on maintaining or enhancing and properly distributing this wealth and the productivity which supports it. This, in turn, requires maintaining the resource base through management of the balance of its materials flows, assuring the sustainability and increasing the efficiency of energy use, and increasing the information content and interconnections directed to meeting the needs and assuring the quality of life of its citizens. Since the information and connectivity are largely held in people, who are constantly changing, the educational processes, by which information is transmitted, are critical to a society's success in maintaining the information balance between generations. Because an eco includes the time dimension, this success can be measured over a shorter or longer time period. A national eco that achieves temporary success by consuming its resource base and accumulating financial and social debt while economizing on education, is condemning itself to long-term failure. As earlier chapters have suggested, our present economic systems fall short of the above definition of success.

Information – the privatization of the commons

While information may be imperfectly reflected in economic determinations of wealth, the boundaries between what is and is not valued and traded are shifting rapidly. With the flowering of information technologies, many people today talk about the coming information age. Information can be accessed and shared with an efficiency never known before. Many businesses see new commercial opportunities in information and are moving aggressively to keep ahead of the competition. Intellectual property rights have become a major issue.

At present, within the Western market system, there is a tendency increasingly to restrict the free flow of information for private gain. Entrepreneurs are exploring every avenue to make money from information, in particular by privatizing it, that is by claiming it as property. Such rights have long been recognized, at least for a limited period, in the form of copyrights and patents, but today the frontiers are being pushed out into new areas of information. One tendency is for cash-strapped governments to sell information and to privatize government services that provide it. This can have undesirable consequences. For instance, scientists researching climate change may no longer be able to afford the meteorological data collected by a privatized weather service, if prices are set to what commercial users like airlines and shipping companies can afford to pay. Government decision-makers may not have the funds to buy the information needed to design proper policies in the public interest. In the context of the theory of ecos, barriers to the free flow of information tend to be dysfunctional, and increase inefficiency in the system. This is similar to the value of free speech in a democracy, where only the most extreme or damaging forms of expression are limited in the public interest.

The recognition of the importance of information flow to the functioning of any ecos requires careful reflection about the concept of intellectual property rights, a cornerstone of modern business. While these rights allow a company to recoup the sometimes heavy research and development costs involved in discovering a new product, and permit writers and musicians to live from their creative efforts, they also tend to interfere with the free flow of information, often to the disadvantage of the poor, who cannot afford to buy it or products based on it. A balance needs to be struck between the right of a person or enterprise to profit from discoveries or creations, and the desirability of allowing everyone to benefit rapidly from new advances. For example, new medicines are expensive because pharmaceutical companies must recover the high costs of research and the extensive trials necessary to prove the efficacy and safety of a product, but the high price prevents many poor sick people from benefiting from the treatment. It is worth asking whether there is any alternative to leaving people to die because only the rich can afford a high-priced medication. This might involve, for instance, retaining some rights for creators, indigenous discoverers and industrial developers to a share of the profits from any use of intellectual property, while leaving the information open to unrestricted use in exchange for appropriate payments, such as through compulsory licensing schemes or charges. The ability to pay may also need to be taken into consideration through some kind of variable pricing.

The move to privatize information, coupled with advances in technology, has opened up a new ideological frontier where a major confrontation is developing. Just as, in the past, other common properties have been staked out, divided up and placed under private ownership, generally for the greater benefit of the already rich and powerful at the expense of poor users, so are claims now being extended to the genetic information that defines and controls all life. Since science has recently provided the means to read, categorize and manipulate this information, it is now being claimed as intellectual property and privatized through patents. However, since only those with enough money can afford the expensive process of patent applications, the poor farmers and indigenous people who often selected and maintained much of the desirable genetic diversity of crop plants, and who discovered many medicinal uses for wild plants, are being despoiled of what should rightfully be theirs. The new Convention on Biological Diversity addresses this problem in principle, but has not yet developed any practical mechanisms to intervene in what could be compared to a planetary gold rush to stake claims to a new area of intellectual property.

The moral issues are even more complex with the patenting of human genetic information, since it is the information on which our own bodies function that is being claimed as private property.

This issue raises not only moral but fundamental economic questions. Is such privatization really in the best interest of economic efficiency and productivity? Where is the balance between free enterprise for private profit and public welfare, which also has its economic benefits? How can the advantages be maximized for the whole society while maintaining the incentives for creativity and innovation?

In the area of agricultural genetics, there are in fact two alternative models operating side by side, one favouring the open flow of genetic information, the other privatizing it. These allow a direct comparison of the two approaches. The research centres belonging to the Consultative Group for International Agricultural Research (CGIAR) have for decades collected much of the genetic richness of major crop plants, pooling it and exchanging it freely so that improved varieties can be tried and adapted to local conditions all around the world. The result has been the green revolution of the past few decades that permitted food supplies to keep ahead of population growth in many places. The benefits were widespread and boosted many national economies and the incomes of millions of farmers, not to mention preventing many famines. Parallel to this, the multinational corporations that make up Western agro-industry have also developed and patented many significant crop improvements, but they have largely been sold to industrial-scale farmers in the wealthy countries who can afford (often because of agricultural subsidies) to buy both the hybrid seeds and the chemical inputs that these varieties require to perform well. In fact, new varieties are increasingly being designed to require the application of chemicals sold by the same multinationals. A significant part of the profit from the higher yield of these crop improvements thus returns to the businesses that own such intellectual property, rather than benefiting the farmers. Genetic engineering is now greatly increasing the possible new combinations of genes, even from unrelated species, and thus the profits to be made. It would be interesting to compare the total economic benefit to society, and the equatability of the distribution of that benefit, between these two approaches.

Apart from the economic factor, there is also a fundamental ecological dimension. It is in the nature of genetic information that its greatest value comes from new combinations. That is what has powered evolution since the beginning of life. From an ecological perspective, the common property approach of the CGIAR permits many more combinations to be tried under a wider range of conditions. This should lead to a faster evolution of new varieties suited to the many environmental situations around the world and thus to both increased diversity and the widest benefit to the world's farmers.

However, the multitude of small farmers and the non-profit research centres of developing countries cannot match the political and financial weight of the multinationals, and access to genetic resources is steadily being restricted. The issuance by the United States Patent Office to private companies of patents covering all future genetically engineered varieties of cotton and soya beans, even those which may be created by others, illustrates the current trend. In response, developing countries are naturally claiming national sovereignty over all their genetic resources in the hope of winning some financial returns for their use by pharmaceutical companies and agro-industry. The barriers are going up and the flow of information will shrink. The theory of ecos shows that reduced information flow is a regressive step, reducing adaptability and productivity in a system. It seems ironic, if not tragic, that these information resources for agricultural improvement are being locked up as 'intellectual property' just when our rapidly expanding population and declining agricultural base threaten to bring major food shortages to the world.

One immediate solution would be to recognize the rights of those, whether scientists in Western laboratories, indigenous peoples of tropical rainforests, or Third World farmers, who have discovered and preserved so much of our genetic heritage and who should be enabled to continue to do so, without restricting the free flow of genetic materials. This could be done through international legislation that would recognize individual and collective rights to both the discovery and maintenance of genetic materials, set their value, and require compulsory licensing or royalty payments from any profits made from the use of such materials, but without restricting the free circulation and use of the materials. The principle would be comparable to rights to a composer's music, which anyone can play, but where royalties are due for any public, profit-making performance. Obviously, it would be even better if the discoverers or inventors of such genetic information would make it freely available as a contribution to the general wealth of humanity, and if their contribution could be recognized in other ways without a cumbersome system tracking uses and collecting payments.

Apart from intellectual property rights, another acknowledgement of the increasing importance of, and value attached to, information in business is in the widespread practice of industrial espionage (stealing information), the confidentiality maintained around commercial secrets, and the headhunting for the employees of competitors who may bring with them inside knowledge. Despite such practices, this type of information is not valued in monetary terms and listed as assets in the company accounts, although it may weigh in the sales price of a business when it is sold. This shows the imperfection of the economics of information at present.

Statistics and measurements

Economics is founded on statistics and measurements. It is not possible to manage a bank account without a knowledge of the balance in the account, the interest rate, deposits and withdrawals. If any one of these kinds of information is missing, management of the account to keep it in the black is impossible. Similarly, economists require basic statistics on the money supply, economic activity, employment, etc., if they are to manage the economy. The same is true of any eco.

However, the financial management on which economics concentrates today, and the monetary values in which all economics is expressed, are inadequate measures with which to manage human society. It is as if we were to try to manage an automobile only through monitoring its fuel supply and consumption, while ignoring its requirements for lubricants, water and maintenance, not to mention the skills and failings of the driver. No matter how well we ensure that the auto always has fuel, we could in such circumstances neither understand nor avoid mechanical breakdowns or driver-caused accidents. Yet such 'externalities' are critical to the proper functioning of the automobile. A more complete accounting system is needed, covering all critical aspects of the eco, whether it be a vehicle or an economy. Such accounts do not all need to be denominated in money. They can be in any units, as long as they permit the calculation of assets and liabilities, the size of flows and their direction (positive or negative). To measure true economic performance, it is just as important to know, for instance, whether the fertility of agricultural soils is stable, if accumulating chemical pollutants threaten future productivity, the rate of scientific discoveries of commercial value, and the trend in skills levels in the labour force. Such factors appear in present economic calculations only when they have an effect on economic performance, which is like waiting for an accident to happen to determine that something is wrong. As shown by the theory of ecos, any monitoring and management systems for ecos must, by their very nature, be multidimensional.

The act of measuring something is often in itself an impetus to do something about it. Unemployment was not a major political issue until unemployment statistics were developed. Once it was measured, governments began taking action to reduce it. A few years ago, some scientists in France developed methods for classifying and calculating noise levels in cities, but a politician asked them to stop their research for fear that, if the inhabitants of the noisiest districts knew how comparatively bad the noise was, they would insist that action be taken to control it. The theory of ecos helps to show the types of factors that need to be measured to understand any system.

Economics and the national eco

Just as measuring something can lead to management, so the reverse is also true; we ignore many things because we have not yet found a satisfactory way to measure them. For example, assume a typical industrialized nation state with a moderate endowment of natural resources, including agricultural land, forests, minerals, oil, a scenic coastline with beaches and an off-shore fishery. When the nation began its industrial development a hundred and fifty years ago, much of the forest was cut to build sailing ships and to provide wood fuel for the new industry. As wood became scarce, coal and then oil were developed as the principal sources of energy for a growing industrial base. Agriculture expanded somewhat to provide raw materials for industry and for food exports, with more recent investment in intensive agriculture using machinery, chemical inputs and high-yield varieties or breeds. Today, with such labour-saving approaches, a much smaller agricultural workforce produces such surpluses that land has to be taken out of production. The over-production, plus competition from imports, drives prices down just when farmers have become heavily indebted to intensify production, while soil quality is declining and inputs must be increased to keep yields up, trapping farmers in a vicious circle of growing debt and shrinking income. Similarly, fishermen have borrowed to buy bigger boats and nets, and now are over-fishing the dwindling stocks in an effort to keep from bankruptcy. In industry, labour has won reduced working hours and higher standards of social welfare, and can now take vacations in coastal tourist centres with many hotels and facilities along the beaches, creating coastal pollution. However, increasing productivity and automation in industry require less labour, so more of the population is becoming unemployed. Much of the wealth of natural resources has been converted into cities and industrial infrastructure.

This is what we consider today to be a successful developed society. However, the reduction in its natural resource capital, the costs of environmental degradation and pollution, and the social impacts of technological change have never been properly accounted for. As the nation's resources run out, it must import most of its wood products, an increasing quantity of petroleum products, and most raw materials for industry. If it is unable to export enough to pay for these imports, it must borrow money in foreign markets, expanding its national debt, which signifies that it is living increasingly beyond its means. Its industrial and urban infrastructure continually depreciates and must be maintained with heavy new investment, but the burden of debt makes this more difficult. Yet by standard economic measures, this is a successful developed economy. In reality, it is an eco that measures and manages its progress solely in financial terms, while depleting its internal resource capital, ignoring the imbalance in external resource flows, and wasting much of its human capital resource. It looks good on paper, but the national accounts do not show the imbalances and the increasing burden of social and resource debt. Its functions are unsustainable and its future survival is in doubt.

If a typical Third World nation with the same endowments started its development only with the collapse of colonialism in mid-century, it will have received extensive international aid, mostly as loans, to develop its primary commodities for export to the industrialized counties. The forests are being exported as whole logs at low prices, and the oil and minerals are exported unprocessed, with little being used to develop local industries. In any case, local wage levels are so low that the domestic market for manufactured goods is limited. A foreign tourist industry has been established along the coast, but the overseas investors who built the hotels import most of what is needed to maintain the life-styles of the wealthy foreign tourists, so most tourism income goes on imports or as profits to the investors. The need to expand export cash crops to pay for imports and to reimburse foreign debt has taken up most of the good land, so local food production has been pushed on to marginal lands where many poor farmers eke out a living while degrading their resources. There has been little real productive investment since much capital has fled the country, and the debt burden has grown as the prices of the exported primary products have declined. The population is growing rapidly, as children are the only form of social security. This is a highly unbalanced eco, rapidly losing its resource capital without corresponding investment, and becoming increasingly dependent on international charity. Its information content is declining even as its population is growing. Many of the poorest developing countries are in this situation today.

Both these situations, reflecting conditions common to many nations around the planet, arise because management and decision-making have been based on narrow economic criteria and measures that ignore sustainability and do not take into account the maintenance of natural resource capital or the maximum use of human resources as required in a sustainable eco. The narrow criteria of financial profitability for corporations or individuals give these specialized sub-sets of ecos the appearance of success, while permitting many costs to be externalized to the whole community, leaving the society itself deeply in debt. Many of the essential interconnections in the system are ignored economically. The real wealth of information content and integration is not valued at all, nor is the transmission of that information through education to ensure the future survival of the national eco. The economic system may seem rational and internally consistent, but it does not reflect reality. It is like living in a dream world, but as with all dreams, we must eventually wake up.

For comprehensive management of human ecos, it is necessary to add information on the balances and flows of natural resources, of human capital and of information as mobilized in human resources. This will require new kinds of monitoring and the development of much more comprehensive systems of national and international accounts. Some work on natural resources accounts is beginning, but human and information accounts that would reflect the capacities, skills, potentials and level of integration of society have not gone beyond the crude data of population censuses and simple human development indexes. Much more work will be required to reflect all essential components of an eco in a set of accounts, either monetary or in alternative measurement units, for those factors that cannot be priced in money terms. The system of monitoring and assessment should be able to evaluate the overall trends and balance in the planetary ecos and in its national and functional sub-units, and to give early warning of major problems in time for an adequate response.

Other economic ecos

The business enterprise or corporation is another type of eco. It can go through a cycle of fragile but energetic beginnings, rapid growth, consolidation and maturity, and possibly senile old age, just like biological organisms and many human institutions. It has its internal capital in buildings, machinery and processes or services, with an import of raw materials and an export of finished products and wastes. It is dependent on outside suppliers and clients with which it must maintain connections. It also has financial flows of income and expenses. All of these must be in balance if the enterprise is to survive. This eco also has its information content in the knowledge and experience of its management and work force, its technical procedures, inventions and processes, that give it its competitive advantage. This information content is appreciated even if it is not accounted for economically, since this is what is targeted by industrial espionage. From a management perspective, a high level of interconnection and cooperation is necessary among the personnel for the business to remain creative, competitive and effective. If a corporation grows, and this is a standard measure of success, then its internal organization must be constantly adapting to new scales of operation, and there may be a size beyond which efficiency and adaptability inevitably decline. As with national ecos, corporate ecos tend to focus almost entirely on the financial accounts, and ignore the balance and maintenance over time of information content and connectivity that is equally essential to their success and even survival. Many big corporations have found themselves in trouble as a result.

The business enterprise is an eco specialized in economic production, just as a chloroplast or mitochondrion within a cell is functionally specialized in energy capture or use. This role is essential, but is only one part of a larger system. The success of the subsystem is essential to the larger eco, but if the larger eco fails, the subsystems fail with it. We need to redefine the place of businesses, especially multinational corporations, in the larger social fabric, to ensure that they are integrated more organically into and responsive to the general needs of society.

Similar principles operate in the family economy. Different members of the family contribute to the eco in specialized ways. In an industrialized country, one or more are usually employed in some external productive occupation that brings financial or material revenue to the family, allowing it to purchase what it requires from outside. The family usually has some capital assets: clothing and furnishings, perhaps a house and land, some means of transport and other possessions. Some, if not all, members of the family contribute services internal to the family for which they are not paid, such as home-making, raising and educating children, which contribute to the well-being, information content and connectivity in the family and thus to its wealth. Families are dynamic units subject to constant change as members are added, grow up and leave it, but they are still subject to the same requirement for balance in material and financial flows as any eco, and have the same potential to increase wealth through information content and connectivity.

A rural subsistence village is another kind of economic system and eco, closely tied to the productivity of adjacent fields, forest and waters. Before the advent of widespread international trade, it would have functioned as a nearly closed system meeting its own material needs, usually with some specialization of roles between families, sexes and age groups. It was generally sensitive to the balance of local resources and had acquired long collective experience in the best survival strategies for its local environment, which were carefully transmitted from generation to generation. Many of these rural ecos have been upset by being linked into larger economies, often not to their benefit. The desire for cash incomes or the pressure to produce for export have often increased pressure on limited resources beyond sustainability. Since there is usually no limit to what can be sold (at this scale), the concept of saving resources for future use vanishes. The quality of life of rural people in the poorer regions of the world is sometimes worse today than it was a few decades ago or even in pre-colonial times.

The global economy

At the largest scale, the global economy can be understood best as a complex nested eco made up of regional trading blocs or common markets, multinational corporations, national economies and many subsidiary units down to the individual farm, commerce and family. Its limits are those of the planet, and its content the fixed resource base of the Earth. Materials fluxes across this outer boundary with space are so limited as to be negligible, making the planet a closed system apart from the renewable energy flux from the Sun, which is essential to its survival. For the global economy to achieve the highest productivity, efficiency and balance, there must be a focus on improved information content, flow and integration at all levels of the system.

Particular attention needs to be given to new types of integration at the global level necessary for maximum planetary human welfare. Improvements in transportation technologies make extensive global commerce and exchange a practical economic proposition. The challenge is to remodel the institutional and legal frameworks to create the careful balance of centralization and decentralization at multiple scales of integration typical of natural organic communities. The central goal of such a system must be to ensure that every inhabitant of the planet benefits, without distinction, from the resulting prosperity.[7]

It is possible on theoretical grounds to define the most efficient economic ideal as a single global trading system with a single world currency and no customs, tariff or immigration barriers, allowing a natural organic balance to become established. However, this will also require fundamental changes in other human institutions and values of the type discussed elsewhere in this book; they are all part of an integrated whole and must be seen as such. To adopt only free trade in the present context of extreme differences in wealth, international economic anarchy and uncontrolled multinational corporations would simply allow the strong to dominate and exploit the weak and increase injustice rather than efficiency. It is necessary both to define the ideal goal and to consider what types of transitional measure would be required to achieve it without undue social trauma.

For instance, the maintenance of many national currencies in the global financial system makes interconnections difficult and causes much information loss, since values are distorted between countries. Denominating all economic exchanges in a single currency will greatly simplify the use of monetary values as a means of communication, reduce costs, eliminate a source of speculation, and maximize the information value of the monetary figures since they will no longer be subject to manipulation for selfish national ends. A single world currency will be like a single world language, facilitating communications around the world. The value of human work and equivalent purchasing power can be used as cross-references for establishing a correspondence of common values between economic systems. Money will still be the common intermediary of reference for goods and services exchanged in commerce, but it will no longer be the full measure of economic performance or development. Other social and information measures will need to carry equal weight in the larger picture.

It has been argued that, rather than a single currency, a world system will require many currencies to provide some protection to distinctive, vulnerable or disadvantaged regions which may need insulation from domination by external economic forces or perturbations.[8] This may well be an appropriate transitional step while some national currencies are still playing an international role, and pending the creation of the necessary institutions to manage an international currency free of manipulation by any special groups or blocs of countries. However, ultimately, this confuses money as a language of trade and as an instrument of economic and social management. The multiplicity of currencies today is one way of maintaining unjust levels of economic difference between countries. It also allows countries whose currencies have taken on an international role to take advantage of that position, while permitting measures they may take for domestic economic management to have often inappropriate repercussions around the world. Transparency, efficiency and justice will be facilitated by a single currency as a neutral unit of exchange, complemented by measures of redistribution or subsidy to compensate for the unequal distribution of resources, vulnerabilities and environmental situations around the planet. The diversity of natural biological communities around the world does not suffer from the common genetic and biochemical bases of biological functioning; on the contrary, it facilitates their enrichment through exchange.

Optimal production efficiency around the world will be obtained by a system of free trade without customs or tariff barriers. This will allow each nation or other geographic entity to specialize in those aspects of production that best suit its natural resource endowments, geographic position and human potential. However, free trade in goods and the free movement of capital are not enough to achieve an efficient balance internationally. The free movement of populations is also necessary to allow each area to adjust to its optimal population density as determined by its resource capacity. If such a globally integrated system is established, balancing efficiency with unity and justice, the economic landscape of the planet will become a network of specialized and interconnected ecos, linked by extensive trading networks of balanced imports and exports, designed to maximize the effective utilization of all the planet's resources for the benefit of the entire world population.

Such a system has major social and cultural implications. While the free movement of capital is already a practical reality, and free trade is the acknowledged goal of countries grouped in the World Trade Organization, the free movement of people is a highly sensitive issue. With the present gross imbalances in wealth and population growth rates between peoples, high unemployment, and deep-seated nationalist and racist feelings in most countries, immigration is a politically explosive question. Only the wealthy benefit today from something approaching a liberty of movement, since economic independence is generally a precondition for visas to most countries, and wealthy tourists are good for business. Economic and even political refugees are turned away at the borders, and chauvinism is on the rise. Clearly, free population movement will be practical only when extreme differences of wealth and poverty have been eliminated, employment is widely available for those who need it, and each culture and ethnic group has sufficient confidence and pride in its own heritage not to be threatened by contact and interchange with other groups, but, on the contrary, to feel enriched by such exchanges. Yet the ultimate goal of the free movement of people around the world must be acknowledged as one expression of justice and equality at the global level. It would be a concrete expression of the concept of world citizenship.

Global free trade will also require harmonized levels of environmental protection and social welfare, so that each area can seek to develop its true comparative advantage, and not simply allow the exploitation of some regions and populations for the benefit of others. Because resource endowments are uneven around the planet, a conscious effort will be needed to increase the purchasing power of poorer areas and groups. Obviously a period of transition will be necessary to achieve this global balance without undue social disruption and increased human suffering, but the present levels of poverty and misery caused by global economic imbalances argue for rapid action. This implies a voluntary sharing of wealth by those who have it in the interests of achieving a more just and stable international system. Some far-sighted countries have already announced their intention to do just this to promote international harmony.

Following the example of natural ecos, the aim should be a global system which encourages and allows everyone to profit from the great diversity of situations around the world for the most efficient production of the goods and services required by the world society and the maximization of total wealth and well-being. To counterbalance the necessary globalization, much economic activity and management will be decentralized to nested sets of ecos at small scales, from the family upwards, where innovation and individual initiative can be maximized. In the context of a much broader definition of wealth and quality of life, local communities may well attribute other values than strictly economic ones to local production and artisanal products, fostering diversity. At the same time, the broad use of natural resources will need some management globally to ensure a just distribution and to prevent external economic perturbations or natural catastrophes from having an undue effect on vulnerable communities. Account will be taken of the full physical, natural and human capital base of the global eco. Productive uses of the natural resource base that maintain or increase the resource capital will be rewarded, while any consumptive or destructive uses will be charged for at the full replacement value for all functions of the resource. All available sources of energy will be tapped to power the global eco and its subsystems in an efficient and environmentally sound way. The production of artistic, cultural and scientific wealth will also be highly valued as increasing the quality of life, as will the sharing of this wealth around the world and its transmission through education to future generations. A new balance will need to be sought between self-sufficiency and interdependence, freed from concerns for national security which will be replaced by global solidarity and collective security arrangements.[9]

Such a global system of production could avoid the pitfalls, both of inefficient centrally planned economies and of a capitalist system where human suffering is often ignored, by replacing the concept of profit for individual benefit by the concept of service to the overall balance of the eco in evaluating economic activities. The profit motive is fundamental to any advancement. It is the selfish profit motive, as glorified by today's economics, that is so damaging, as well as being morally destructive to the individual. It can be replaced, through education, by an altruistic profit motive, a desire to benefit all of humankind, the individual included. This same adjustment will be appropriate in businesses and corporations. Corporate aggrandizement should be transformed into corporate service to benefit the whole community.

The 'trickle-down' theory of economic development, which stated that profits to the wealthy would eventually trickle down to benefit everyone, has been largely discredited. It is not an automatic mechanism. Too many of the wealthy simply expatriate their profits to foreign bank accounts rather than investing in their community. The redistribution of wealth can be implemented best by the principle of voluntary sharing, cultivated through education, whereby the desire to amass wealth is replaced by the desire to share it through philanthropic action and assistance to the poor. This will become a 'free-enterprise' approach to social welfare, which could have the same advantages of flexibility, innovation and efficiency over a centrally planned social welfare system as free enterprise in private industry has over a centrally planned economy. Some combination of the two, complementing voluntary charity with graduated taxation and governmental social security, is probably most desirable, but this will only work with the necessary moral transformation in society.

In such an economic system based on broader human values, financial profit will become just one measure of balance and efficiency among others. The real focus of individual performance, corporate business performance and even government or national performance will be service to the community or society in general, as represented in the healthy financial, resource and human accounts of the eco. That service might be the provision of a material product, a social service or an increase in information value and interconnection. From this change in values, new social and institutional structures and procedures will follow naturally, and the economic system will become more socially responsible without undue coercion or regulation.

It is this change in values and units of measure, from a money-centred system to an information-centred system, where the real value is in being of service to others, and where the profit to the whole is more important than profit to any one component, that can provide the social mutations to make a new kind of productive economic system possible. The change would not be so radical, since most economic activity, whether in agriculture, industry or the tertiary sector, does aim to provide needed goods and services. It is the efficiency of doing this that needs to be measured and valued, both in a broader system of social and economic accounting, rather than just financial profit and loss as is done today, and in comprehensive accounts for the whole society or eco, rather than just for a few businesses or individuals.

The above vision of a global economy based on transformed values can easily be dismissed as utopian and unrealistic, and the gap between the ideal and the real world of today is admittedly very large. On the other hand, economic systems do not stand still, and the difference between, say, the advanced social welfare state of the present day, the raw industrial society of one hundred years ago, and the feudal regimes of earlier centuries is also very large. The changes in Europe over the last half-century of the European Union are a good example. It would thus not seem unrealistic to aim to achieve a fully functioning global economy in fifty to a hundred years, and to identify a series of transitional steps that could move economic structures and practices in the desired direction. Society can probably still choose between two paths. We can adopt a conscious and directed evolution of the Western economic system, pushing the pace of change as rapidly and widely as social conditions allow to close the gap between rich and poor, or we can let ourselves drift through a more irregular and painful transition with periods of blockage, refusal or inability to change, leading to major crises which finally precipitate significant advances. Unfortunately, the movement of society towards world peace since the beginning of this century has been following the latter pattern. Recession, depression and financial and industrial collapse are the economic equivalent of world wars.

Some argue that there should be no global economy, but that independent and sovereign national economies should continue to be the only units of economic management. This largely governmental perspective is founded more on the wishful thinking of political leaders than on economic realities. Multinational corporations and institutional investors already recognize the planetary scale of economic activity and behave accordingly. They may prefer their present freedom from international regulation and global taxation, but society must sooner or later bring this back into balance, just as it has done at the national level. Some enlightened companies and investors are beginning to realize that global stability and predictability are in their best interests.

Scarcity and population

The possibility of achieving an improved and more human organization of society at the global level is only a recent phenomenon. For most of history, the great majority of humankind were poor and had to labour to meet their basic material needs. The skills needed for survival were passed from father to son and mother to daughter, or through more collective educational processes within the extended family, tribe or community, and this limited the technological and productive capacity of the society. As civilization developed an increased information capacity, technology and specialization made production surpluses possible. Today, it is the ability of a shrinking proportion of the workforce, using increasingly complex information and technologies, to produce goods that meet all our material requirements, that is changing the ground rules of economics. What we are seeing is the emergence of technologies which can bring to an end that scarcity in the necessities of life which was one of the original driving forces of our present economic system. Enough food, shelter, basic health care and education can be produced for everyone. Unfortunately, present scientific and technological efforts are not being focused on global priorities for such basic welfare, but are too often diverted to secondary, trivial or unproductive ends. Even so, the technological possibility to saturate markets and end material scarcity has already been achieved for some social groups in some countries. Scarcity and poverty can be a thing of the past. The limitations are economic and social, not technological.

However, the elimination of scarcity will not be realized generally as long as the human population continues to grow out of control. The danger is that the scarcity, formerly imposed by limited technology and human productivity, will be replaced, through our reckless population expansion and profligate waste, by a new scarcity imposed by the lack of adequate primary resources and the reaching of planetary limits. There is a clear trade-off between the number of people this planet can support and the ultimate standard of living of each individual. A smaller total global population will mean a larger per capita share of planetary resources.

Uncontrolled or excessive population growth, in both the developing and some industrialized countries, is threatening global stability because the number of people is growing faster that we can provide them with education, employment, or the resources to meet their own needs. The masses of the poor are deprived of knowledge and of ways of connecting into, and becoming productive parts of, society. This impoverishment in information is probably more significant and debilitating than material poverty, because education and the ability to access and use knowledge can give people the tools to help themselves and to create their own wealth. At a time when international development assistance programmes are increasingly being questioned and cut back, it may be worth reviewing the relative effectiveness of information exchange as opposed to financial transfers for achieving lasting development. Investments in education and communications may contribute more to resolving the problems of poverty than building dams or factories. The demands for the transfer of technologies are, in reality, demands for the information that technology represents. What is needed is less the gift of a computer, which has a limited life, but a transfer of the knowledge necessary to make, master and use computers and other technologies, and that knowledge is needed not just in books, but in people. The latter is a prerequisite for the former.

The number of people is not the only dimension to the problem. The quantity of resources required to support each person is equally important, and this varies greatly depending on the living standard and life-style. The present per-capita consumption of resources in the industrialized countries is so high that it is draining resources from around the world. The poor cannot compete with the purchasing power of the rich. Essential resources required for survival in the South are diverted to the non-essential needs of the North. A significant reduction in the present levels of consumption in the industrialized countries will be needed to free resources for basic needs elsewhere, in order to keep within the sustainable capacities of the planet. This is not a problem that can be resolved by the operation of a market system. In fact, it may be aggravated by it. It requires alternative approaches to economics in which unity and justice are basic operating principles.

The cancer of power

Any proposal for economic and social change must address the issue of power, and how it is held and wielded. The present dysfunctional economic system is basically an expression of the values held by those who hold power and wealth in government and the private sector. Kings and aristocrats, politicians and industrialists have competed for centuries, in war and in peace, for their personal benefit as much as for any more general interest. The principle was even enshrined in Adam Smith's 'invisible hand'. It is only natural that such leaders would adopt systems catering to their needs. Yet in terms of ecos, the self-centred lust for power and wealth is like a cancer, drawing resources to itself for its own aggrandizement while ignoring the natural systems, checks and balances that allow the organism to function most effectively. It makes human social ecos less healthy than they would otherwise be, and if unchecked and allowed to go to an extreme can be fatal.[10] Rulers have all too often placed heavy burdens on their subjects to raise the means to go to war against their neighbours, at incalculable human and economic costs, so as to build or defend their power. The economic system has often just been another tool to these ends.

Yet what else is an economy for if not to meet the needs of people? It is not so that politicians can glory in the strength of their

Gross National Product, and use it to throw their weight around in the world. Values, in a narrow materialistic sense reflecting the importance of power and wealth, are inherent in the unconscious foundations of modern economics. They have just been taken for granted and seldom questioned, because to question them would be to shake the foundations of the whole system.

From the perspective of human ecos, this tendency to dominate by a few leaders seeking power restricts the development of the full potential of available resources, both material and human. It excludes many from full participation in the system, and thus limits the efficiency and productivity of the ecos. The enormous wastage of people in modern society is an evident result of the imbalances produced in the system by such concentrations of power. The redistribution of power in more organic structures and mechanisms can help to resolve this problem. A change in consciousness on the part of the leaders and of society as a whole is also necessary.[11] Some of the means to do this are discussed in the next chapter.

Notes

1. Schumacher (1973).
2. See, for instance, Ekins (1986); Robertson (1989).
3. Henderson (1988); Daly and Cobb (1989); Costanza (1991).
4. Daly and Cobb (1994).
5. See the very interesting Bahá'í International Community statement on *The Prosperity of Humankind* (1995).
6. Daly and Cobb (1994).
7. Bahá'í International Community (1995).
8. Robertson (1989).
9. For further development of this theme, see the Universal House of Justice (1985).
10. I am grateful to James Robertson for suggesting this analogy.
11. Russell (1994).

CHAPTER 7

Human capital

Any blueprint for change must consider all the human dimensions of society. It is not sufficient to plan for the physical needs of the population, through economic development, without also considering the values and emotions that drive each individual. Human dignity, cultural richness, spiritual growth, community acceptance and recognition, a sense of self-worth and usefulness to others are as important as, if not more important than, having sufficient material goods. Development as a social goal must be able to include all these and not just the financial flows measured by GNP or per-capita income.

The theory of ecos highlights the importance to the whole system of information content and connectivity as reflected in such human dimensions. In social and economic ecos, that information is largely held by, and functions through, people. The theory therefore requires that we re-examine the place that human capital, including people and their values, acquired knowledge and experience, is given in the management and evaluation of socio-economic systems.

Human dimensions

The human organism is at the evolutionary apex of biological development. We may not be the fastest, largest or strongest organism on the planet, but we are clearly the most intelligent and adaptable, and have become the dominant species around the world. It is thus useful to examine the evolutionary mechanisms that have produced this particularly successful organismic eco.

Physical evolution through biological processes is relatively slow. Since the emergence of *Homo sapiens*, the present human species, there has been some superficial differentiation, for instance to favour darker skin in sunny tropical countries, and pale skin in northern climates where small areas of skin need to absorb maximum sunlight in order to manufacture vitamin D. Such minor differences have had no impact on the organic unity of the human species, as evidenced by the extensive and continuous interbreeding around the world. Indeed, population mixing and the advances in medical science have largely eliminated physical selective pressures, such that natural selection through premature mortality and differential reproductive success has probably been largely replaced by random drift. Physical evolution is not a significant factor in modern society.

Humans are distinguished from other organisms by a highly elaborate information storage and processing capacity, often referred to as our power of reason or intelligence. This has been favoured by evolution, leading to an organism in which the potential intellectual capacity is still far from being utilized effectively. As a result, the intellectual evolution of society has become a cultural rather than a natural process. Science, technology and the arts are some of the mechanisms through which this evolution is taking place. Cultures that encourage and invest in these processes can advance more rapidly today than those that do not. This dimension now dominates the development of human social ecos.

There is also an emotional and spiritual dimension of humanity that is less well understood and appreciated. It is seldom considered in an evolutionary context, if it is considered at all. Yet here as well there is evidence of powerful evolutionary forces. Many major advances in civilization have been driven or accompanied by important religious transformations and advances in human values. Moses taught simple laws which revolutionized the tribal level of organization. Christianity was born into the well-organized Roman Empire, and thus did not address matters of social organization (render unto Caesar that which is Caesar's) but brought radical new values for individual development and salvation to make personal relationships more human. Muhammad gave warring tribes and diverse peoples the values that welded them into the first modern nations. The evolutionary progression in values and the resulting social organization is evident. One reason for a scientific resistance to consider evolution in a religious context is that the principal mechanism for change, described in most religions as Divine revelation or spiritual enlightenment, escapes any scientific explanation. The result, however, is clearly of great significance to the development of human society and ecos.

The above mechanisms all concern the collective social evolution of humankind. They have allowed the progressive development of various scales of eco from the family and tribe to the village, city, nation, and now towards a world society. There is also an important set of evolutionary stages in the development of each individual person. We start with physical development towards a mature adult, accompanied by extensive intellectual development that can continue throughout a lifetime. There is also a level of moral and spiritual development, moving from self-centred animal- or child-like reactions towards other-centred behaviour and the acquisition of moral qualities. This latter dimension is particularly important in favouring improved relationships in human social ecos, and will be discussed in some depth in this chapter.

The value of people

Human beings are complex and highly evolved ecos, with not only physical requirements, but also emotional, intellectual and spiritual dimensions that are important to their individual functioning and to their social relationships and higher levels of organization. Part of the problem with valuing people and their place in society rests in the weight or importance given to these different dimensions. The animal dimension, including our basic physical needs such as for food and shelter and our ability to provide physical work, is often emphasized, particularly in relation to the poor. Meeting physical needs is clearly fundamental for survival, but survival is not the only thing that makes us human. Our intellectual capacity is also increasingly recognized for its economic value and its contributions to society, as it is the primary tool for information storage and exchange. The emotional side of people is often neglected, although it is critical to human motivations and the relationships that determine social organization. Emotional levels of communication are significant but poorly understood. The spiritual dimension of humanity is ignored or denied by some, and seen as primordial by others, but is generally totally disregarded in economic analysis and policy-making, although it often underlies the framework of values within which economics operates. Given the importance placed on each of these dimensions in at least some cultures, it is reasonable to consider them all in an integrated analysis of the human system.

There have been debates down through history over humanity's place in the natural world, and in social and economic structures. At any time, the conclusion has depended primarily on the dominant values and the consensus view of the nature of humankind. Where people see themselves as particularly aggressive and cunning creatures in search of power, warfare has pitted one group against another in a constant struggle to dominate. Those for whom this world is simply a difficult but necessary passage towards another one that is more spiritual and desirable may have little motivation to invest in this one. At times when people have been seen primarily as productive labourers in the society, the role of the worker has been highly valued and everything structured around that role. Since humans are complex creatures, some mix of these viewpoints has usually influenced groups and individuals within the society.

This is an area where religion, philosophy and political theory have had profound effects. It is also fundamental to any understanding or interpretation of economic and social systems, for they can only be judged for their adaptability and efficiency in terms of the underlying values of the society. For instance, suppose we take as the underlying principle that human beings are potentially malleable and productive machines which can be moulded to our economic requirements. As with any machine, they age, become rigid, and wear out. As new ones are produced, preferably in surplus to keep costs down, we select the best and train them to fill vacancies in the productive apparatus, according to the needs of the moment. If one breaks down and cannot easily be repaired, we toss it out and replace it with a new one. As our productive needs change, we discard the old workers and replace them by new, cheap, freshly trained ones, or by machines if labour costs are sufficiently high. Everything is valued in terms of the efficiency of the productive machinery, keeping costs to a minimum. What happens to people before or after is of little consequence.

An eco structured to this materialistic set of values would put a premium on worker productivity, but would otherwise have no concern for human welfare. If the above sounds familiar, it is because it is in fact the value system of the principal economic entities of Western society, whether private corporations or public enterprises. Businesses are today the most powerful social units, together with governments and the military, yet they are held accountable primarily for their financial productivity as reflected in their balance sheets. Social welfare is the quite separate domain of governments and charities. When governments legislate to limit extreme exploitation of workers and to share the social burden, it is only because the external costs imposed by business on the society at large are too high. The capitalist system is founded on a very narrow view of human value as labour, combined with a Darwinian concept of survival of the fittest. It assumes that failure and wastage are part of the natural order of things, and are necessary to maintain economic efficiency. A certain level of unemployment is considered desirable to keep wage levels down. If businesses fail or people are poor or unemployed, it is their own fault for being less competitive. This is, in fact, a way of avoiding moral and financial responsibility for the larger social damage caused by the workings of the market and of specialized economic structures like corporations in a narrow economic system. It is a major source of discontent and social stress.

The logical if extreme conclusions of such values and lines of reasoning, that prefer political or economic goals over people, can be seen in the excesses of Nazi Germany, the 'ethnic cleansing' in the former Yugoslavia, and many other situations around the world. All are symptoms of the bankruptcy of morals and values in modern society.

The irony is that many well-off people today are touched by pictures of African famines and feel that no one should be allowed to starve to death, while at the same time complaining about the free-loaders living on welfare when they should be working, and supporting a free enterprise concept that implies that only the fittest should be employed. They accept each position independently without recognizing the fundamental contradictions between them. It is for this reason that a more integrated approach, considering all aspects of human life, is required, rather than the compartmentalized situations so common today.

We need to rethink how society should deal with individual and group failure. In biology, survival of the fittest means that the unfit do not survive. In business, it is considered normal for an out-dated or poorly managed company to be taken over or go bankrupt. However, to adopt the same attitude towards people and to kill them or leave them to die would be morally unconscionable, precisely because we accept that there is an intellectual and spiritual dimension to people that warrants great efforts to preserve human life. It should be unthinkable today in industrialized countries with ample resources to leave the poor to starve in the streets, or to abandon the mentally or physically handicapped. But those who fail to find employment, who are marginalized or drop out, are too often judged differently. Somehow their failure is seen as their own fault, a sign of laziness or corrupt behaviour. The poor of the Third World are often considered the same way, as somehow responsible for their plight. Such people are seen by many to put themselves beyond the obligation to solidarity. These attitudes are a symptom of moral escapism or myopia, of a refusal to face up to uncomfortable facts that may imply a need for real sacrifice and change.

The human dimension must be returned to its central place in our concept of society through the recognition of the importance of human capital in the functioning of all social ecos. Furthermore, people must not be considered as one-dimensional producing and consuming machines, but in all the cultural, social, emotional and spiritual complexity that determines their functioning in society.

Information and people

Human beings are distinguished from all other organisms by their mastery of information and its intellectual manipulation, illustrating the dominant evolutionary trend towards greater information content and connectivity in ecos at the organism level. Our complex language, rational faculties and powers of abstract thought have given us the ability to manipulate and dominate the natural world for our material and economic betterment. This usage has paralleled our social evolution towards increasingly complex communities and societies in nested sets of socio-economic ecos.

Humans are thus the information creature *par excellence*. While modern computers may now calculate faster than people, our ability to collect, store and manipulate information in creative ways is still far beyond any machine we can manufacture, and even computers have been created by us as tools to extend our data-processing capacity. Our power over nature and our scientific ability to use nature for our own purposes come from our reasoning ability, which is an information function. We are the inheritors, depositories and transmitters of science, culture and all other aspects of civilization. Our capacity to record, store, recall and reuse information, either within our brain or by extension in external media, has given us the ability to create an ever-advancing civilization in a global eco, building on the progress of those who came before by increasing the information content we pass on to future generations.

At the same time, we are mortal as individuals, with an allotted lifespan and an inevitable cycle of birth, youth, maturity, old age and death. Each of us accumulates information throughout our life. We are educated and trained in our youth, and then use that information and experience to contribute in some way, large or small, to society. We continue to acquire skill and knowledge, both expressions of stored information, throughout much of our life. As we have children and raise a family, the process of information transmission begins again, perpetuating language, culture and values from generation to generation. The creativity inherent in human nature gives each of us the potential to add something to the information we pass on, and that accumulation of additions, whether a new recipe for beans, a musical composition, an improved method on the shop-floor or a major scientific discovery, is what builds civilization. Inevitably, much information is lost with the passing of each individual. Yet the strength of a civilization lies in its ability to preserve and transmit a rich, coherent and useful body of knowledge and experience from many individuals to many other individuals. Civilizations as distinct ecos rise and fall as their collective information content grows or declines.

From this perspective of the theory of ecos, the most valuable component of a society is its knowledge and information, and much of this information is stored not in libraries, databases or bank accounts, but in people. In fact, information stored in books or digital codes is latent and inactive; apart from some computerized systems, such information only becomes productive when it is mobilized in people, and then incorporated through them in products and systems which they design and operate. Of what use is a computer diskette crammed with data if there is no computer to retrieve that information or system to use it? What is the value of a library if no one reads the books? Such stored information is only a potential resource, not a productive one. Information becomes useful when it is expressed or applied in people or in other functioning systems or ecos.

Much practical information is, in fact, stored only in people, and directly transmitted from generation to generation. For instance, a skilled traditional boat-builder would have learned the trade as an apprentice from older workers. Many were able to build boats of a proven traditional design without plans. If such boats went out of fashion and young workers stopped learning the trade, such information would be entirely lost. The same is true for many farmers' knowledge of their fields, their traditional crops, the weather and other useful information. Most of this has been lost with agricultural modernization and changing education.

Each culture has its store of information. The supposedly 'primitive' people of Pacific islands such as New Caledonia in fact had highly sophisticated agricultural systems and knowledge of their environment.[1] Each village might maintain thirty different genetic varieties of a major crop plant like taro or yams, each adapted to a particular climatic situation or part of the garden. They constructed elaborate terraced irrigation systems despite the rugged terrain, transporting water over long distances through the mountains. Their houses resisted cyclonic winds that would flatten many European buildings. Specialist holders of knowledge, such as the Master of the Yams or the Master Fisherman, maintained a hereditary information base and advised the village when to plant or harvest, and where and what to fish. Unfortunately, because their intellectual frame of reference was different, such people were considered sorcerers by the early missionaries. One particularly tragic and symptomatic story was of a skilled village surgeon and sculptor, who, upon conversion to Christianity, lost his skill with the knife and never practised again. For him, this skill was not his own, but a gift from his ancestors; when he gave up his belief in the intervention of his ancestors, his talent was lost.

In another context, the US government recently launched an oral history project among the scientists and engineers who built the atomic bombs, because they recognized that the masses of documentation and detailed plans in their files did not contain all the practical information that would be needed to do it again if necessary. In general, only the successes were recorded; no one wrote up the mistakes, the dead ends, the solutions that were tried and failed.

The human capital of accumulated knowledge and experience is undervalued in today's narrow economic approach. People are not paid salaries based on their total value or knowledge; it is only a limited number of services that they can render that enter the market place and are priced as employment. The result is an enormous waste of human capacity, and a gross inefficiency in the use of human resources. The social pressures building up today from this wastage threaten to overturn the very foundations of our society. Industrialized countries invest in education – that is in filling people with information – because a well-trained workforce is seen as economically valuable. Yet when it comes to using those resources in the workplace, our processes of recruitment are haphazard and inefficient, we tolerate a constant wastage along the way through unemployment, and then retire at an arbitrary age those with the most experience in order to lower personnel costs and to increase opportunities for younger workers. The many people victimized by these processes represent that much lost potential to generate wealth for society.

This human wastage results from the narrowly defined compartmental structure of our present social ecos, and the limited ways in which the success of some of those compartments is measured. The sub-units specialized in economic productivity (corporations, businesses, multinationals) are divorced from those with social responsibility (governments, families, charities). For the former, social costs are externalities and the principal driving force is returns to investors. Yet most governments are deeply in debt, if not almost bankrupt, in part because of the weight of their social responsibilities, whether for education, health, unemployment or retirement. The tensions between the wealth-generating and wealth-consuming components of society (as wealth is narrowly defined in today's economics) are constant. These imbalances between institutional components are growing as the productive sector becomes more capital intensive and sheds labour. The proportion of the population in productive employment is shrinking as people live longer, educational requirements for the young increase, and rapid economic and technological change create more unemployment. Yet it is businesses and their workers that must, through taxes and social charges, pay for all the rest. This fundamental structural problem places great stresses on the consensus on which any stable social order must be built.

The problem needs to be considered in quite different terms. If knowledge and information are accepted as the real wealth of civilization, as suggested by the theory of ecos, then new types and levels of organization will be required in human ecos to use and develop this newly recognized information capacity. This will, in turn, require new kinds of principles and laws to guide the evolution of the many types of social eco towards increasing integration and complexity. Since information at this level is managed, manipulated and interpreted by people, these principles and laws must operate at the level of people, whether singly or in groups.

Two kinds of knowledge

The knowledge that underlies the organization and development of society can be grouped within two general frameworks. Science deals with the reality and operation of our physical world, while religion, broadly defined as the basic value systems shared by a community and underlying most past and present civilizations, addresses the moral and spiritual dimensions of human nature. The two are basically complementary, with one explaining our material world, and the other telling us how to live in it. Both help to situate us in our physical and social surroundings.

Science is both a body of knowledge and a rational method of exploration and discovery. It is characterized by a devotion to truth, a quality that can be beneficial everywhere in society. One of the strengths of science is thinking in terms of process, of the dynamics of a system. The theory of ecos is a typical application of this approach. Evolution is the extension of that study of dynamic processes over time to trace the changes and historical development of a system. It is a powerful scientific concept for explaining and understanding the natural world, human history, and our own individual development. These scientific concepts are as appropriate to religion as they are to any other aspect of life. Religion is also concerned with the truth, involves process, and evolves over time both as a social phenomenon and an individual experience.

Today, the mastery of science and technology is unevenly distributed around the world, being generally concentrated in the most prosperous and industrialized countries. It is, in fact, largely used to maintain the technological and economic supremacy of those countries, and thus contributes to the growing gap between rich and poor. Yet science is universal wealth, part of the common birthright of all peoples. It should not be the preserve only of an educated elite, but accessible to, and used by, all of humanity with the necessary capacity.[2] Centres of learning, devoted to the generation and application of knowledge, should become an essential component of all communities, forming an institutional structure central to the purpose of all human social ecos. The new electronic information technologies and communications networks are making such a decentralized approach to science a practical possibility, by facilitating interchange between scientists and access to libraries and other sources of scientific knowledge. The widespread sharing of science and technology on an equal basis will do much to reduce the extremes of wealth and poverty in the world.

Religion provides an essential complement to science, preventing it from sliding into pure materialism, just as the rational approaches of science can help to protect religion from falling into the equally dangerous trap of superstition. Religion tells us how to use science for our benefit. It gives us the basis for value judgements, moral choices and applications that are beyond the realm of science. For science, nuclear bombs and nuclear power plants are equally valid applications of scientific knowledge. Genetic manipulations will soon allow us to correct birth defects or clone identical human beings, but science will not say what is desirable and what is not. The many misuses of science in the recent past demonstrate the need for a moral framework as a counterbalance to the power of the scientific method.

Civilization has the best chance to advance sustainably when there is a continuing constructive dialogue between these two branches of knowledge. The theory of ecos provides a conceptual meeting ground for these two powerful forces in life.

Functional values

Values provide the basic rules governing human interactions. They indicate what is good or bad, desirable or undesirable. They determine whether you love your friends and hate your enemies and competitors, or, as Christ taught, you love your enemies as well. Nationalism, racism, consumerism and altruism are expressions of certain kinds of value. Values may have a rational component: i.e. it is good to stop at a red traffic light not only because the law says so, but because I may be hit by another car if I ignore it. However, they are frequently founded on beliefs or emotions that are not subject to rational questioning. They are often assimilated unconsciously within the family or society, and can thus be difficult to articulate, confront, and change if necessary.

In the biological world, there is no real equivalent to human values. Animals are generally governed by instincts that allow them to recognize their own kind, and other organisms with which they must interact, and know how to behave towards them. They usually recognize without training a predator they should flee from, a prey they should eat, or a partner they should mate with. Sometimes there is also a learned component, as with infants who imprint on the first creature they interact with, usually their mother, but exceptionally with other species or even a human. But regardless of the imprint, their behaviour towards 'mother' is instinctive. With unfamiliar creatures, they may learn by experience if they are threatening or innocuous, desirable to eat or noxious, but this is still not equivalent to human values which have a greater degree of abstraction. We value a stove not by whether we can get burned by touching it, but for its usefulness in cooking our food.

Similarly, relationships between other organisms, no matter how elaborate, are not governed by values. There is no reason to suppose that lions think 'I like gazelles because they are so tasty' or that a malaria parasite is in any way conscious of the host that it is exploiting. Many organisms have mutually beneficial or symbiotic relationships that have developed simply because they have evolved together. Concepts like selfishness, greed or forgiveness simply do not apply outside of the human context.

What is in fact remarkable about the human species is how little instinct remains. A human infant is totally helpless and must learn almost everything. The rare examples of abandoned or sequestered children cut off from normal human contact suggest that we have no innate values; they are all acquired in one way or another. One consequence of this is that, without acquired values, man is worse than the animal, which at least is controlled by its instincts. Wanton violence and killing are rare in the animal world, but only too prominent features of our own. When a society neglects to transmit an adequate set of functional values, it can easily slip into a spiral of decline and disintegration.

Values can be acquired in many ways. A mother plays a crucial role in forming the values of her infant and in guiding its development through childhood. In many cultures this role is shared by an extended family. We may simply observe and mimic the behaviour of others, whether as a child, or as a traveller may do in an unfamiliar society. Direct experience helps in forming some values, and probably in confirming many others, as it may also lead to rejecting some inherited values that seem to conflict with reality. Formal instruction plays an increasing role, whether in a religious context or, too rarely, in schools. The institutions of society also contribute, including by rewarding some kinds of behaviour and punishing others. It is thus apparent that any adult's framework of values is the result of many and varied influences. The crucial factor is that values are acquired, and that this process is thus amenable to modification and improvement.

Values are significant in the theory of ecos because they condition and determine the interactions of people and thus the information flows within and between social units. The rules of human interaction result from a complex interplay of culture, example and education, but ultimately they are founded on the attitude of each individual towards others, an attitude that is largely emotional or even spiritual. The emotional spectrum of people ranges from base selfish desires to altruistic self-abnegation, from the infantile to the mature, from the material to the spiritual. Negative values can block information flow and constructive interaction, while positive values can facilitate more effective human ecos. One of the goals of civilization has always been to move individuals up the emotional spectrum, acquiring what are seen as more human (or even Divine), as opposed to animal, qualities. It is those human qualities of honesty, trustworthiness, love, forgiveness and generosity, to mention only a few, that bring people together and help them to function in complex communities.

As civilization evolves and the information content of complex human social systems increases, the values and principles underlying social behaviour become codified in a framework or structure. These can range from more brutal and rigid social codes in simple societies, such as 'an eye for an eye and a tooth for a tooth', to more flexible and dynamic laws and principles which the social systems must apply to their own organization if they are to advance. Some of these value systems emphasize an internal frame of reference through the development of the individual conscience and sense of responsibility. Others refer to an external source of values and enforcer of judgements. In most religious systems this is God, Allah or an equivalent figure. In some secular societies, it is the king, ruler, dictator or high priest who takes on this role, often, unfortunately, primarily for self-aggrandizement. People then may suspend moral judgement and blindly follow whatever the ruler decrees.

Today there is a need for a new, more adaptive set of values as the environment of our global eco is changing. For instance, if technology makes it unnecessary to have to work to survive, then we should be educated to want to work to be of service to society. There is a basic latent human need to be of service, and to have a constructive place in society, that is evident, for instance, in the frustration of the unemployed on welfare or of people who are forced to retire. Modern society is much more complex and large-scale than anything known before, and we have access to much more information about each other. We therefore need to value unity in diversity, and to become more accepting of human differences of all sorts. In particular, we have become conscious of the process of our own collective development, and we thus have both the potential and responsibility to plan and guide our further evolution as social ecos.

Sources of values

Values can originate from many sources and undergo various transformations. Some may form through a slow process of social evolution, representing collective human experience derived from trial and error. The widespread condemnation of incest, for instance, may have originated in the observation of frequent abnormalities resulting from such in-breeding. Other values may result from a conscious intellectual effort, such as that represented by the work of philosophers, or the observations and deductions of scientists.

In almost all societies, fundamental sets of values have historically been provided through what can best be called religion, whether one of the great revealed religions, a religious philosophy, or a traditional set of beliefs passed down from the ancestors. It is, in fact, religious values, as they have been renewed and extended from time to time by the great religious leaders or prophets, that have been what could be called the social and spiritual mutations in values necessary to drive the cyclical process of rising and declining civilizations that have marked the path of a slowly evolving and progressing human society. The earliest remaining historical traces of this are in the story of Adam and Eve and the discovery of good and evil. Many indigenous peoples tell of a great ancestral leader or spirit who brought the rules or values for their society. Moses brought the concept of law and simple justice in the form of an eye for an eye and a tooth for a tooth. The Buddha referred to a spiritual plane of existence more important than this earthly life, and the path of good conduct that would lead there. Christ introduced to the Roman Empire a revolutionary concept of love and forgiveness, turning the other cheek. Muhammad taught submission to the Will of God (Allah) and to the collective benefit of society, moral principles that underlie the modern nation. Bahá'u'lláh emphasized justice and the oneness of all humankind. The Prophets have all said that their inspiration came from outside of themselves, through a process of enlightenment or revelation. The fundamental similarity of their messages would suggest the commonality of their source. While there is no way to assess these claims scientifically, their impact is undeniable. Religious belief is probably the single most powerful source of human values, either directly or by assimilation into the general value structure of a society.

Despite the frequent emphasis in religion on love and brotherhood, differences in values or in the systems supporting them have often led to conflict. Wars of religion, inquisition, intolerance and fanaticism have scarred the history of civilization. One result has been the trend to the separation of church and state and the secularization of society. Another has been the divorce of science and religion as two mutually incompatible intellectual frameworks. As a consequence, religion, as a source of values and a social force, has been increasingly neglected by the powers in society, as something irrelevant to the modern world. This is particularly the case in business and economics, which, in a sense, have replaced religion as the central driving force in present Western civilization. However, despite the material power that this civilization represents, its advocates are only a minority of the world population. Globally, there is probably much more openness to the role of religion in society. While the powerful force of religion in society has often been discredited by extremism and by its manipulation for political ends, its potential for constructive transformation, as attested by the historical record, cannot be ignored.

In recent decades, a new process has been set in motion by governments through various negotiations of an international consensus on values. The United Nations Charter and the Universal Declaration of Human Rights are examples of the international codification by governments of universal values. Numerous international conventions also aim to fix values in international law, such as those regulating forms of warfare, establishing the rights of prisoners of war, banning genocide and chemical weapons, or protecting the rights of workers. Every international conference produces a Declaration which fixes agreed principles, rights and obligations concerning the subject under discussion. This process of legislating human values through governmental and intergovernmental processes underlies a major shift in influence from religious to secular authorities even in religion's own domain. It is one response to the fragmented and often antagonistic state of the diverse religious traditions in an increasingly united world.

Changing values

Any attempt to apply this analysis of ecos constructively to human society must address the need to change underlying values from those that militate against the effective functioning of ecos to those that work in their favour, such as by reinforcing a sense of world citizenship. Effective human relationships are the foundation of all the other changes that are needed for any social ecos to evolve constructively. Without improvement at this most fundamental level, any alterations will only be cosmetic. If we can get the basic rules of human interaction right, then the development of new kinds of collective social ecos will follow naturally.

To begin with, we need to stand back and look at our basic assumptions. Are human beings really fundamentally aggressive, power-hungry, selfish, and lazy, or are these simply some among many human characteristics, perhaps even abberations resulting from economic circumstances or up-bringing, which can therefore be modified or replaced through education?[3] In the absence of moral education, people can be dominated by self-centred and aggressive tendencies. One of the symptoms of the malaise in presentday society is the evident lack of morality and self-control everywhere. As a consequence, social cohesion is weakening, where it has not, in extreme cases such as Rwanda, Somalia, Liberia and Afghanistan, collapsed altogether. Only a remoralization of public and private life will be able to reverse this trend. But what proof is there that such a transformation is possible on a large enough scale, and what mechanisms can be used to bring about the changes required?

While knowledge plays a central role in human life and society, it must be accompanied in each individual by the motivation to make use of it in ways that are constructive. Motivation may have an intellectual component, but it is rooted in personal emotions and values. Building effective social ecos requires close human interactions that will be determined as much by attitudes and feelings as by objective information. In particular, if change appears threatening or requires sacrifices, the emotional inertia to be overcome will be great even if the long-term interest in change appears clear. Resolving the problems in our present human ecos will require approaches that reduce the prejudices, tensions and hatreds that keep people apart, and strengthen all those forces that unite people in efficient, cohesive groups.

Ultimately, it is spiritual and moral belief that, if properly directed, brings to each individual a transforming power able to overcome selfishness and inertia and to provide the courage and motivation for change. There is a universality in the core values of all religions and many other value systems. They all teach a turning outward from the self towards a higher reality, and cultivating positive feelings of love for others. They emphasize the golden rule of doing to others as you would have others do to you. Moral qualities like honesty, truthfulness and trustworthiness are common to every tradition. These are the foundations for feelings of solidarity and altruism that make other-directed change possible.

There are, in fact, many past examples of rapid changes in basic value systems which demonstrate what change is possible. Some of the best cases occur in the early history of religions. The changes in the idol-worshipping tribes of Israel that Moses instigated, those that the Buddha introduced to India and China, and those that Christianity brought to the secular, hedonistic and increasingly corrupt Roman Empire are some examples, as is the transformation by Muhammad of the warring and brutal tribes of Arabia into a civilizing force that swept from Spain to the Philippines. Secular examples of major social transitions accompanied by changes in values include the French Revolution, the rise of communism in Russia, and the spread of Western materialism by commerce and the media in our own time. The large-scale mobilization of nations at war or after national calamities shows that people can be shaken out of their apathy and moved to action. Some combination of perceived threats and enlightened or charismatic leadership is usually required. Even then, public opinion may take time to shift, as demonstrated by the efforts of American leaders required to convince public opinion in the United States to accept its entry into the first and second World Wars. Such changes are much easier to see in retrospect than when they are experienced directly, yet they are, in fact, still taking place. With the impact of modern media and widespread travel, the process is probably even more rapid and extensive today than ever before.

Change is even possible in those aspects of human behaviour that have been so widespread as to seem inherent in human nature. The individual drive for power and status is one value set often identified as the source of many social and political problems. While there is clearly a personality component in the desire to dominate, inter-cultural comparisons suggest that the major contributor is education. Many educational systems reward those who seek power, and most political systems and many businesses select for those who want power and who are prepared to go to considerable ends to get it. Media stereotypes reinforce the desirability of these behaviour patterns. Changing this in order to adapt to the requirements of more balanced organic forms of governance for ecos will require both modifications in the approach to education, and changing the structures of politics and government, for instance by separating the charismatic inspirational function from the administrative or legislative function, and by replacing self-selection by community selection. There will always be a need for leadership in most social ecos, but the form that such leadership takes and the way it is exercised can be adjusted through careful institutional design and new educational approaches. For example, the drafters of the United States Constitution over 200 years ago failed to agree on an ideal structure for society, and instead adopted rules for making rules in a system with sufficient checks and balances to neutralize the worst extremes and temptations of human nature in the exercise of power.[4] The result has been an evolutionary social system with amazing resilience relative to other systems of government of the same time.

There is now almost no limit to the material goods the wealthy can accumulate, but those goods clearly do not equate with happiness. The consumer society has created a cult of material possessions in which changing styles and planned obsolescence drive an excessive and conspicuous consumption for short-term economic benefits. Yet the psychological stresses produced by this extreme pursuit of material success and status are readily apparent. The high levels of violence, drug abuse, suicide, alcoholism, mental illness and consumption of tranquillizers and anti-depressants in many materially affluent communities are symptomatic of the failure of wealth as such to bring satisfaction or happiness. As a result, the principle of a reasoned moderation in life-style is an attractive alternative. Possessions do not equate with quality of life, once basic needs are met. Learning to decide when we have enough is another potential goal of education, even if such a concept of contentment runs contrary to the modern consumer mentality carefully cultivated by advertising. This change in values can help to moderate the excessive consumption of the industrialized countries, which is a principal cause of global imbalances and a barrier to solving the problems of poverty in the world.

For the poor, obviously, it is first necessary to ensure the minimum physical requirements for life, such as food, clothing, shelter, health care, and education. It is only when people are freed from the struggle for existence that they can concentrate on fulfilling the other aspects of their human potential. Emphasizing the values of moderation and contentment among the wealthy, combined with a recognition of the oneness of humankind and the resulting necessity for solidarity and voluntary sharing, should facilitate the transfer of resources necessary to enable the poor to meet their basic needs and to join in the building of a more just society.

If human worth is no longer to be judged by material possessions or social status, then the alternative is to strive for distinction through the refinement of human character and spirit. Since character includes those qualities of openness, understanding, freedom from prejudice and concern for others that raise the quality of human interactions, this will help each individual to participate fully and constructively in the ecos of which he or she is a part. The content of education will thus take on new dimensions to favour both the perfection of the individual and the advancement of civilization. Education will serve to transmit those values that will permit modern social and economic ecos to function effectively. The foundation of all this will be a sense of global consciousness and citizenship, so that each member of the human race will be motivated to acquire the skills, knowledge and values necessary to contribute effectively to an increasingly interdependent world.[5]

Eco-values

The need for new or renewed values and moral principles addressing the problems of modern society has been widely recognized. Even such early studies as *The Limits to Growth*[6] noted the importance of human values and called for new goals and commitment. US Vice-President Al Gore, in his book *Earth in the Balance*, addresses this problem, reviews the approaches of various religions, and calls for a 'Global Marshall Plan' against poverty and underdevelopment.[7] The exemplary work of Daly and Cobb,[8] one an economist, the other a theologian, combines a creative rethinking of economics and a consideration of the underlying values that should accompany it.

The question has always been how to achieve this. There are many groups and scholars that are creatively exploring the values that are needed today. Some, such as the Foundation for the Progress of Humanity and the former Group of Vézelay, which together produced a Platform for a world of responsibility and solidarity,[9] and the Club of Rome with its series of studies and reports, have taken a lay approach. Others have worked within various religious and moral traditions. The Catholic Church has issued a series of encyclicals on social issues, starting with *Rerum Novarum* in 1891, that have developed a considerable body of church doctrine that apply moral principles to the major concerns of society,[10] on the basis of which the economic dimension has been explored further.[11] Examples of a Protestant approach have also been developed.[12] Outside the religious traditions, others have taken a more humanistic approach, emphasizing the learning of values, humanistic psychology and self-actualization,[13] or looked at values from the perspective of poor developing countries.[14] These are only a few examples.

One of the most coherent sets of what could be considered 'eco-values' necessary for the operation of a global human eco can be found in the principles proposed by Bahá'u'lláh, founder of the Bahá'í Faith, over a hundred years ago.[15] He emphasized such moral concepts for the individual as a dedication to the service of all humankind, preferring others to oneself (it works if everyone does it), the importance of honesty and trustworthiness as the necessary foundation for social interaction based on mutual confidence, the elimination of all forms of prejudice, etc. His central social concept was the importance of unity, based on justice, as the principle to govern all human relationships. He coupled this with social principles such as universal education linked to an individual responsibility for investigating truth, the need to balance science with moral and religious values, the necessity of an international auxiliary language to facilitate communications, the importance of wide consultation and participation as the basis for social decision-making, all in support of the ideal of world citizenship. He said that we should regard humanity as a human body, such that if any part of the body suffered, the whole body suffered. He emphasized economic concepts such as the need to apply spiritual solutions to economic problems, including adopting values of moderation, contentment and detachment from material things, elevating work to a spiritual obligation equivalent to worship, advocating the voluntary sharing of wealth and a sense of responsibility for the poor, and eliminating extremes of wealth and poverty through such mechanisms as a graduated income tax and basic support for those in need. His institutional prescriptions included an elected consultative system of administration (described further in the next chapter) and a call for a federated world government with executive, legislative and judicial branches and provisions for collective security. Taken together, these values and concepts contribute to improved information flow, relationships and connections between people and social units, and provide some guiding principles for the operation and evolution of human ecos towards a world society.[16]

Similar moral and ethical values can be found in all the great religions and many ethical movements. The Ten Commandments of Moses, the straight path of Buddha, the moral principles of the Baghava Gita, the teachings of Jesus and Muhammad, the wisdom of Confucius and Lao Tse, the high ideals of personal behaviour in many traditional beliefs of the native Americans, Africans and Pacific Islanders, the principles upheld by humanists, all call for high standards of individual behaviour in the interests of society. The golden rule of love and charity finds its expression in all the great religious traditions.[17] Such values could be likened to the lubricant in human relationships, smoothing interactions and facilitating a high level of connectivity in society.

There is, in fact, a significant convergence of these many paths towards a common set of basic values reflected in the examples cited above. That does not seem to be the problem. Where we have fallen down is not so much in the principles themselves but in their application, and it is here that a major effort is needed to reinstil in society a belief in the importance of values and in the need for each individual to put them into practice in his or her own life as the first essential step towards a better future society. We need a revival of individual moral standards as the basic rules for the operation of all human ecos. It is only by transforming the values of people as the central elements in our economic and social ecos that we shall be able to bring the planetary human system back into balance. Such a fundamental shift in the ingrained thinking of most people will be difficult but not impossible, as history has repeatedly demonstrated. The challenge of our transition to a world society is thus fundamentally one of education to a new set of values.

Education and human capacity

Education, including both the formal and informal processes by which a person acquires language, skills, knowledge and values, is the key to information transmission, and thus to the functioning, survival and renewal of any human eco. It plays two fundamental roles. It prepares each person within an eco to carry out the particular roles through which they can contribute to society. It also ensures the survival and perpetuation of the eco beyond the lifespan or functional term of each individual within it, by passing essential information from generation to generation. In addition, it is something entirely under our control, even if that control can only be exercised gradually and organically as generations succeed each other.

Education is critical both to the development of the information handling capacity of each person and to social apprenticeship. From the beginning of life, we learn how to relate to others and to function in society. Even in animals, many aspects of behaviour, some quite fundamental to survival, may be learned through experimentation or observation of the actions of others, rather than be determined by instinct. The human family was, and still is, the first educational unit, providing for children during the long dependency required for their physical, social, intellectual, moral and spiritual maturation. An infant must learn just about everything, from language to sexual behaviour. Much of this education is informal in the family or community, with many aspects of language, culture and social comportment simply perpetuating themselves from generation to generation. Only a small part, largely intellectual development and occupational training, falls within the formal educational system and school curriculum.

The fact that so much of our behaviour is learned does give some hope for the possibilities of major change in society. The kinds of aggressive, power-seeking, self-centred and hedonistic traits that so mark our own time are not inherent characteristics of human nature, but simply some of many options possible, or even the result of an absence of adequate education in certain domains. At different times and places in history, and in different cultures, there have been marked variations in the dominant characteristics of human behaviour. There is no reason why we cannot make conscious efforts to channel our characteristics more constructively. Thus the most effective channel to implement fundamental changes in society is through education, broadly defined to cover all aspects of transmission of information, values and forms of behaviour.

Unlike physical traits, which are fixed by genetic inheritance, acquired social characteristics can be transmitted, at least in part, from generation to generation. Young people may rebel against their parents, and must experience many lessons over again for themselves, but they still tend to fall into patterns of behaviour that they have learned from those around them. Thus each person who succeeds in transforming his or her life, in ways more appropriate to successful ecos in the modern world, also contributes an example for others to follow. The multiplier effect of this transmission by example can be considerable over time.

Revisions in formal education can also make a major contribution to social change, as illustrated by head-start programmes and others to overcome some of the consequences of racism in America. Social transformation can be accelerated most rapidly by the education of girls, because, as mothers, they are the first educators of the next generation, and will thus pass on to all their children the values, behaviour and knowledge they have acquired.

The power of education to transform society should not be under-estimated. With the inevitable turnover of generations, the general adoption of curricula fostering a sense of world citizenship and of values facilitating improved human interaction, and thus the operation of ecos at various scales, would result in the complete reorientation of human society within half a century. An historical example of this process at work was the work of Jules Ferry in late nineteenth-century France. The French Revolution had brought political change, and then reaction, leaving enormous cleavages between revolution-aries and reactionaries, and resulting in social and political instability. Ferry's solution as minister of education was to establish a system of universal free compulsory public education teaching republican values. The result, within a generation or two, was a more harmon-ious and stable French society.[18] Ferry is still widely remembered in France today for this accomplishment. Therefore, this scale of social change is technically within our means. It is the political will and motivation that are presently lacking.

The implementation of any programme of individual and social transformation, such as that required for a more economically and ecologically balanced and organically structured society, will require rethinking the education of children both at school and in the family. It is not enough to learn to read, write and calculate; there must also be education for good character, not in any sectarian sense, but through inculcating the values necessary for successful functioning in the community. It should not be too difficult to agree on a basic set of universal values, such as honesty, justice, and compassion, shared widely by the great majority of religions, philosophies and cultures, and to set them within the context of world citizenship. Many are already incorporated in international declarations and covenants. Governments, non-governmental organizations, and all those involved in the exploration of renewed sets of values, as described in the previous section, should work for their incorporation into whatever educational processes are available to them.

While the challenge of reorienting the educational systems of the planet seems immense, much could be accomplished with some far-sighted political will. One hopeful fact is that the technological transformation of the means of production has been paralleled by a revolution in the means of education. Just as printing freed us from the limitations of hand copying, so have electronic media freed us from the physical transmission of printed pages. While there will always be a need for that human contact and interaction that can adapt education to the special requirements of each individual, not to mention meeting other social and emotional needs, the potential for access to knowledge is no longer limited in time or space. The role of the teacher will be less in communicating knowledge than in adapting its transmission to the needs of the learner. Teaching will, in fact, become one of the most important and respected roles in society. Universal education is now technically possible at a speed and with a detail and richness never before possible, and this opens the possibility of the full participation of every individual in the real wealth that is information. Information is the only kind of wealth that is not diminished or lost but is increased by being shared.[19] Education provides the tools for increasing information and other kinds of wealth. It empowers people to take charge of their own destiny and development.

Involvement

Educating the individuals in society is only the first step in the process. Once they are equipped with the necessary knowledge and motivated with an appropriate set of values, they must have the opportunity to use their skills and potential through active involvement in various types of eco. Each person is born into certain social ecos, including a family, community, cultural group and nation. In addition, he or she will pass through ecos associated with different stages in life, such as schools or military service, and will choose to join additional ecos providing employment, social activities, religious fellowship, etc. These affiliations are not necessarily permanent, and can be changed with greater or lesser difficulty. All these social ecos can provide opportunities for a person to fulfil some of their potential to contribute wealth (information, knowledge, experience, beauty, culture, etc.) to society.

Today, our neglect and devaluation of human capacities has resulted in a tendency to take power and responsibility away from people and to concentrate it in hierarchies and bureaucracies. As education has become concentrated in the schools at an ever-younger age, parents have abdicated their responsibility to their children. People in industrialized societies depend more and more on government to care for the handicapped, clean up the environment, improve agriculture, save failing businesses, and establish norms for every aspect of their lives. This attitude is even reaching to the farthest corners of the developing countries. When a small remote village of a South Pacific island was in danger of being washed into the sea as waves carried away the sand on which it was built, the villagers were asked why they did not make a rock wall along the shore to protect their houses. They replied that they did not because the government would not pay them to do it. The result of this process is not only a growing dependency, but an institutionalization that loses touch with local conditions and reduces the initiative, efficiency and adaptability of society. Ecos that over-centralize and enlarge become rigid and inefficient as information flow is retarded or blocked and connectivity is reduced.

Similar problems arise with the cult of expertise. In too many fields, there is an assumption that only those with the right training, degrees and diplomas can make any useful contribution. Even highly educated people hesitate to step outside their own discipline, and may be severely criticized if they do so. Insiders defend their professional prerogatives and 'maintain standards'. Conversely, in other contexts, particularly in developing countries, only the outside expert is to be believed and followed; local expertise is considered inferior and suspect. Clearly, there is a delicate balance between the need to ensure quality in fields like medicine and engineering and the tendency to maintain a closed shop for other reasons, generally selfish advantage. Society will advance more rapidly if there is a wider use of human potentials and more openness to alternative approaches, creative solutions, and the common sense that comes from practical experience.

For example, the success of methods of participatory planning has shown that even illiterate rural villagers understand the complexities of their local environment and are perfectly capable of monitoring the changes taking place in it and planning for the most effective use of its resources.[20] While they may use seeds, stones or fingers for counting, and draw maps on the floor with chalk, the plans they produce, based on first-hand knowledge and accumulated experience, are often much better than those produced by highly trained (and well-paid) outside consultants or experts in government departments. Yet there has long been a tendency to take such responsibilities away from local communities and to give them to government bureaucracies. Where help may indeed be needed locally is in ensuring the widest possible involvement of all parts of the community in local planning and decision-making, including women and youth, and not just traditional leaders, land-owners or power structures. This requires mechanisms for consultation and participation that improve information flow and interconnections within the community, so that its full human capacity can be drawn upon and all interests are communicated and considered.

Local communities, organizations and individuals can also become directly involved in the environmental monitoring and other collection of information necessary for effective decision-making. There are developing initiatives to involve non-governmental organizations, school children, and even religious institutions in such monitoring.

An interesting example of the better use of human capacity through involvement is that of the Brazilian manufacturing company in which employees set their own salaries and working hours, elected and evaluated their own bosses, set their own business targets and controlled their own expenses. All had access to and could understand the company accounts, knew what everyone else earned, and took part in major business decisions. Since most employee earnings were tied to profits, and budget controls were strict, there was strong peer pressure not to abuse these freedoms. The system worked because it recognized and used the capacity and initiative of all its employees, and all could see their individual interest in the success of the company.[21]

Putting people first

An analysis of the human component of our modern social ecos shows that there are two fundamental and interrelated flaws. One is in the institutional substructure of ecos. Social units such as businesses and corporations do not value, and are not accountable for, the larger interests of society, or even for the people within their own ecos. Furthermore, there is no overall system of accounts to demonstrate the imbalances among the sub-units. This aspect will be discussed in the next chapter. The other flaw is in the valuation itself, where humans are peripheral to the central economic interests of society despite their being the primary repositories of its information content, and ultimately the intended beneficiaries. We have so undervalued people that we have developed a money-centred society rather than a people-centred society, losing sight of the fact that social and economic structures should exist for the benefit of people, and not the reverse. We pay lip service to the principle, as in 'We the people of the ...', but our actions often show the contrary. This is not to say that narrow economic principles, monetary accounts and balance sheets are wrong, as has already been noted, but only limited and incomplete. We need other kinds of analysis and management, based on a more holistic people-oriented perspective, to give a complete view of the functioning of our ecos.

Drawing on the example of complex ecos in nature, it is possible to sketch out the characteristics that human social and economic ecos should have in order to operate and evolve more organically and to make better use of the potential of all people to acquire, increase and perpetuate the knowledge and information that is the real wealth of civilization. Since human resources (people), and the information they hold, are the most important part of our resource capital, the goal will be to maximize their knowledge, interaction and productive use, just as the key to the survival of a complex ecosystem is the maintenance of the full complement of its component species in all their complex interactions.

The basic economic question thus changes from: how can we maximize the efficiency of material wealth creation with minimum human and capital inputs? to: how can we maximize the total wealth produced for the whole society making best use of all available human productive potential? Unemployment would be like throwing away money. Automatic retirement would also be a waste of resources. When work was seen as a necessary evil, involving the exploitation of workers for their labour, retirement was a social benefit, but if work is revalued as an opportunity to be of service to society, then arbitrary retirement is a privation of social, psychological and spiritual advantages and a senseless waste. It is a change in the type of service, rather than an ending of all service, that may be appropriate at different stages in life. If the goal is the most efficient and productive use of human potential as required by the application of the theory of ecos, then we need to break out of the present rigid framework of careers and employment, making it more flexible and adaptable to both human and economic necessities.

A similar situation occurs in natural ecosystems such as coral reefs. It is in the interest of each plant, or animal with symbiotic plants inside, to be as efficient as possible in absorbing the energy of sunlight and converting it into food energy, getting the maximum output for minimum input. However, it is in the interest of the whole coral reef system to make the maximum use of all the incoming light energy, even if many organisms are only contributing the slightest net increase under marginal conditions. The result is the complex form of the reef, with many surfaces to catch as much reflected light as possible, and many kinds and layers of organisms, right down to boring algae living within the rock itself to catch the last glimmers of light that succeed in penetrating the many layers above. In this way, the reef supports the maximum richness of life and maintains the high overall productivity of its ecosystem.

Just as today's economics tries to maximize national product, revenue, material capital accumulation and the return on investment, so more balanced social ecos will try to maximize the creation of new knowledge, and its accumulation and transmission through people. Every effort will be made to use all the available human talents to contribute to wealth creation (both material and intellectual) and to social services, particularly those that increase human well-being (and thus productivity) and the transmission of information to succeeding generations. We know that only a small percentage of human intellectual potential is presently being used, but only a much more intensive life-long process of social interaction and education will make it possible to develop this potential more fully. An effective social eco will aim for the highest overall standard of living and productive involvement for all members of the society, with a constant process of mutual enrichment through improved information exchange.

The use of the full potential of each individual within the eco will probably result in a reduction of individual specialization and an increase in the diversity of individual contributions. Even the most highly expert and specialized people today reach a point of diminishing returns in their work, as evidenced by the growth of hobbies, recreation and vacations as means of re-establishing some semblance of balance in life. By making many processes of learning, research, communications and decision-making potentially more efficient, technology has in fact freed much human capacity for other uses. The idea of the Renaissance man (or woman), able to do many things well, will come back into fashion. There is no reason why people should not strive simultaneously for artistic, intellectual and material excellence. A mix of physical labour, intellectual activity, social service and contributions to education will be healthier, and psychologically and socially more rewarding, than the present compartmentalized life in Western civilization, with narrow occupations, where people lucky enough to have employment probably have less free time than in any period of history. This will also fit with the reduced labour requirements in industry and agriculture brought about by technological increases in productivity. The participants in such an eco could have several part-time activities or occupations, in a mix that could change throughout life.

The concept of a people-centred knowledge-oriented society of many interrelated ecos responds to a new social situation. The recent revolutions brought by communications, transport and information-processing technologies and the phenomenal increases in labour productivity have changed the context radically from that addressed by Karl Marx in the last century. Labour can ever more easily be replaced by capital, and the resulting excess labour produces chronic unemployment. Economic justifications to create jobs are no longer sufficient. We need jobs because it is individually and socially beneficial to work, and doing so maximizes the total wealth produced by and for society.

Ecos aimed at the greatest total realization of human potential will change human relationships in fundamental ways. There will still be some competition and a striving to excel, but the motivation will be different. Instead of efforts to block or hurt competitors in a desire to beat them to the reward (which assumes that rewards are limited and only the strongest will survive), there will be more impetus to share in the progress, as each advance by others will be beneficial to the whole eco. This is already the principle underlying basic scientific research, for instance, where the accumulation of information and understanding is the fundamental goal. The free sharing of information through publication is the accepted ideal, so that the results can be confirmed and extended by their replication by other researchers. In this sense, the scientific community is a model for society. This is a logical consequence of the shift from a focus on material wealth, which is inherently limited, to knowledge as wealth, which is not diminished but in fact enriched by sharing.

For similar reasons, all other forms of exclusion will be eliminated in human-oriented ecos. All inequality, prejudice and gender bias that exclude some groups from full participation in society and from the fulfilment of their human capacity represent a significant loss in potential wealth production. The inequality of opportunity to which women are subjected in many cultures already handicaps half the human population. Add to this other forms of prejudice based on race, culture, language, class or religion, and only a small minority can be considered today to have every opportunity to become fully productive members of society.

Many women with extensive training and experience are unable to return to their career after an interruption for raising a family, and experience deep frustration at their unfulfilled potential. Many refugees have gone from being engineers or university professors to being manual labourers or taxi drivers. Social disruption only increases the human tragedy. The wastage of human talent and capacity caused by this system of bias and exclusion is phenomenal. The ecos of a human-centred society, on the contrary, will draw fully on the richness of human diversity, where many complementary qualities can reinforce each other.

The waste today is even greater among the masses of the poor, who are never even given a chance to develop their potential. Their mental capacity may be stunted by poor childhood nutrition and environmental conditions; educational opportunities are minimal or entirely lacking, as are the resources that might permit the development of some skill or talent. An enormous effort will be needed to break the vicious circle of poverty and to allow all people to begin to fulfil their human capacity.

Responsibilities of society

The revaluing of human potential and human capital to favour its maximum sustainable use will require fundamental changes in the operation of society as we know it. Service to society will be recognized as a fundamental human right. It will be the responsibility of social ecos to provide everyone with the opportunity to develop some kind of talent, and with the means of using that talent to contribute to society and to earn a livelihood. There will need to be mechanisms to help individuals identify the ways in which they can best contribute to meeting society's needs, to provide them with the necessary training, and to match them with requirements. Since both those requirements and each person's capacities can be expected to change over time, occasional readjustments will be required. As people age, their capacities for certain kinds of activities, such as those requiring physical exertion, may diminish, but their potential as teachers, for instance, with valuable experience to pass on to younger persons will increase. If maximizing the return on human

potential and experience becomes as important as return on investment is in the economic system of today, the capacity of society
to create and transmit knowledge, which is one of the principal
functions of human activity and essential to the survival of all human
ecos, will increase considerably.

A much better exchange of information will be required to match
those seeking positions with the positions available and the services
required by society. The efficiency and flexibility of a market system
may have its place here, through some kind of human skills market
based on the value of each person's store of information and
experience. There will be more focus on the whole person with
many abilities, and not just on one talent or capacity. There could,
of course, still be areas of specialization, but these will be developed
and combined in many ways suited to the diversity of human
capacities. Concepts of career and success will change drastically, as
will individual motivation. While there will still need to be differences
in material rewards, depending on the type and quality of the services
rendered, this will become less important than other types of satisfaction. A 'safety net' of community support will be required only
for those unable to support themselves, such as orphans, the very
elderly, the ill or the extremely disabled, as well as those in temporary
need from crop failures or natural disasters, or while changing jobs.
The society will place a high value on holders of knowledge, skills
and wisdom, and teaching will become one of the most highly
respected occupations because of its fundamental role in the
transmission and continued use of the information, skills, culture,
attitudes, values, and world-view that are the most fundamental
wealth in the society.

The concept of remuneration for services performed will need
to be re-examined in the larger social context. While today only
certain kinds of work are paid, while other equally critical services
such as subsistence agriculture and the work of a housewife in home-
making and raising children are not, such injustices will need to be
eliminated. This does not necessarily mean that housewives should
be paid (although this might be a transitional measure). The whole
concept of work as a service to society, as related to mechanisms
for the sharing of wealth and benefits, will need to reflect the new
values of society necessary to ensure the optimal functioning and
usefulness of the productive ecos.

A more humane society that values the family as the basic social
eco and the first educational environment for children will also stop

considering individuals in isolation from their family situation. The geographic transfer of an employee, for instance, can force major sacrifices on a spouse with professional commitments or other responsibilities, and on children at sensitive points in their education and social development. If family unity and well-being are considered important within a more integrated view of the overall interests of the eco and its members, then all these factors will naturally be considered and be subject to consultation before such important decisions are taken.

Business and employment

Ecos directly involved in material production, such as businesses and industries, will come to recognize the complementary nature of material capital, human capital and information in their enterprises. Business ownership will no longer be limited as it is today to the providers of financial capital. This idea is already receiving limited recognition in employee-owned companies and by the inclusion of company shares in executive remuneration packages. The extension of this principle will transform labour relations and lead to the expansion of such practices as profit sharing with workers and much wider participation of employees in the ownership and operation of the business.

The requirement, in order to maximize the use of human capital, that society provide everyone with opportunities to earn a living, coupled with the individual moral obligation to work and a prohibition on idleness, will eliminate unemployment as presently experienced. Anyone leaving a job, either voluntarily or from restructuring, will be assisted to find a new position appropriate to their capacity and experience, including the creation of new job opportunities if necessary. The assurance of alternatives and help during transitions will encourage more employment flexibility and job mobility in a way that would be advantageous both for businesses and for workers. Losing a job will then no longer be threatening, as it is today. This will also greatly simplify institutional change, since today most people resist such change because of the fear of losing their employment. Since levels of consumption will be maintained even when businesses have to shed workers, the cycles of boom and recession would be dampened. More thought needs to be given to the mechanisms to finance employment creation as part of a general review of the uses of national wealth. Since modern society already accepts that no one should die of starvation and exposure and is ready to make the necessary means available through charity, emergency aid and social welfare programmes, it is not such a big step to convert charity into a working wage.

Again, these proposals amount to a radical reorientation of society as we know it and question the very foundations of our economic system. There will be resistance to change from governments, business and the labour movement, but as the number of jobs continues to shrink and the social pressure for solutions to poverty and unemployment grows, ideas such as these can be expected to make rapid progress. Some experimentation will be necessary to find the best alternative formulas and institutional structures. Once such approaches have been tried in a few more venturesome and socially concerned countries, they can be expected to spread rapidly.

Accounting for human capital

The revaluing of human capacity, talent and ability to serve society will also lay the foundation for a new kind of accounting to complement monetary and resource accounts. Communities will need to measure how well they are using their human potential, as well as their success in accumulating and transmitting the many kinds of information that are a culture's true wealth. For instance, instead of the negative measure of unemployment, there could be accounting of all the many ways human talents are being used in the community in productive and creative activities (perhaps in person-hours or years devoted to each activity). A society could then judge its efforts in agriculture, industry, education, arts and culture, science, sport, environmental management, health care, etc. To monitor the transmission of knowledge and information, some measurement of the educational levels and accumulated experience of each generation will be required, including the effectiveness with which older members recorded and passed on their store of wisdom, skills and experience before they died.

A set of common human measures will provide a standard for global accounting, with 'equal pay for equal work' as a basis for reducing the present extreme differences between industrialized and developing countries. There is no rational reason, apart from the self-interest of the privileged and an intellectual inertia bordering on paralysis, for an hour of the same kind of work to be valued differently between countries or regions. If any differentiation is appropriate in valuing material obligations, it could be between city and village dwellers, with less expected of those living simpler lifestyles close to the land than of those with the greater opportunities, responsibilities and material means available in urban areas.

The labour force will thus be defined as the entire human population, and all human activities which serve society will be considered important, and accounted for, regardless of how or whether they enter into the 'cash economy' as presently understood. A new 'human capital' economy will take its place. The goal will be the maximum productive use of all the human skills and knowledge in the society, contributing to the full intellectual, moral and spiritual development of the human race. The definition of the kinds of service valued could be adapted to each community's circumstances and culture, with great diversity possible around the world. Such measures for the better use of human potential will provide the basis for a new and more just balance in society.

With the development of tools and methods for evaluating the status and trends in human capital, a more balanced approach to the management of human ecos at all scales becomes possible, ensuring their continuing evolution. The administrative and institutional structures responsible for the direction and management of local and national communities, and of businesses and other productive units, will be able to follow their progress in developing and utilizing all the potential human capacities available to them. They will be able to compete for the best skills, and in their efficient employment of the human resources available, just as businesses today compete for capital and the highest productivity. The pressures for efficiency and innovation will be the same, only the currency will change from money to people. They will also be able to manage the continuing process of transmitting knowledge, skills and values from generation to generation. They will thus be able to maintain the balance of their eco, while assisting each individual in the refinement of his or her character and in contributing to an ever-advancing civilization.

Notes

1. Dahl (1985) gives a more complete and documented description of this example of traditional environmental knowledge.
2. Bahá'í International Community (1995), IV.
3. Universal House of Justice (1985).
4. Artigiani (1993) p. 34.

5. Dahl (1990).
6. Meadows et al. (1972).
7. Gore (1992).
8. Daly and Cobb (1989, 1994).
9. Distributed by the Fondation pour le Progrès (1993).
10. Biffi (1989); Weigel and Royal (1993).
11. Miller (1994).
12. Duchrow (1987); Daly and Cobb (1994).
13. Lutz and Lux (1979).
14. Tévoédjrè (1978).
15. See Chapter 1, note 2.
16. For a further development of Bahá'í approaches to the environment, see Dahl (1990).
17. Schnapper (1952) illustrates this with a compilation of quotations from the different scriptures.
18. For an excellent biography of Jules Ferry (in French), see Gaillard (1989).
19. Raine (1993) shows how arts and culture are not diminished by being shared.
20. Participatory rural appraisal and similar methods have been described in Lamb (1993).
21. Ricardo Semler, described in *The Economist*, 26 June 1993.

CHAPTER 8

Organic communities and institutions

One of the remarkable features of the human species is its propensity for elaborate and varied social organizations. Just as the first reproducing molecules combined into cells for their own protection and efficiency, and cells combined into multicellular organisms of ever-more-elaborate types, so have organisms gathered together to form communal ecos ranging from the loose-knit gatherings of song birds to the highly organized social insects like bees and ants. The many species have further combined into complex communities and ecosystems. Human communities are distinguished from those of animals by their diversity and their multiple levels of organization, made possible by their high information content and complex communications. Our societies are also distinguished from natural ecosystems by our extensive domestication, management and modification of other species for our own benefit, through agriculture, forestry, horticulture, aquaculture and biotechnology.

Human social organization is basically a mechanism to group and to increase the interconnections, direct and indirect, between members of a society for particular functional purposes. It is the form and structure of the organization that define any particular human eco and embody a significant part of its information content. In a family or village, for instance, individuals will know their defined roles and place in the community, which determine their positions in the hierarchy of rank and leadership, their operational functions, and their relationships to other members. There may be written laws, plus generally accepted codes of conduct, often unspoken and almost unconscious, which are learned in childhood or by observation and imitation. These defined interrelationships and channels of communication within the eco maintain a certain stability despite the constant changing of roles as children grow up and become parents, elders die, and people assume a succession of different responsibilities in the hierarchy. They permit the social eco to perpetuate itself and to provide essential functions to its members.

The theory of ecos shows that functional units tend towards an optimal size, either by dividing to maintain a constant size or by adding multiple levels of organization with nested or interconnected substructures, or both. Human society illustrates this tendency well, whether at the family, community or institutional levels. A corporation, for instance, will grow to the point where its management structure becomes inefficient, when a reorganization will divide it into a series of subsidiaries or profit centres within a larger and looser corporate framework. As a city grows, satellite neighbourhoods or suburbs spring up, creating a smaller scale of community life. The process is a universal characteristic of organic organization.

The new technological environment

As civilizations develop, the kinds, frequency and information richness of human exchanges within them increase, often structured through forms of government, community and institutional organization. For most of human existence, there have been limits imposed on the size and scale of human communities by our capacities to collect, store and communicate information. Before the invention of writing, oral traditions were preserved in human memories, which both placed a ceiling on the amount of information that could be preserved and transmitted, and resulted in a certain amount of change or drift in the collective memory from generation to generation. Sometimes physical objects or pictograms may have helped as reminders of essential features of such traditions. For instance, certain rituals in the Solomon Islands required recounting the genealogy of the priests of the family line; the skulls of the priestly ancestors were kept in baskets on shelves in the custom house to facilitate this task. Perhaps cave and rock paintings served similar functions.

Writing increased the scale and accuracy of the information recorded, but it still had to be manually copied. For inscriptions engraved in stone, the reader had to come to the writing. Even more portable media such as clay tablets, parchment and papyrus had to be physically transported on foot, by horseback or by sailing ship, so few had access to the writing and dissemination was slow. Printing allowed wider copying and distribution, increasing access, but not speed. Most present human institutions first took form under these conditions of the social environment. The priesthood or clergy of many religions, for instance, were originally the only literate members of the community, charged with reading the rare copies of the scriptures and teaching them to the masses. The churches and temples, with their sculptures and paintings, and accompanying rites, were the audio-visual supports for the educational lessons in community morality and tradition for largely illiterate worshippers. The impact of Chinese, Jewish, Greek and Roman civilizations was particularly lasting because of their literary traditions; their great authors are still read and quoted today. The word in its written form took on particular importance in Islam, the first religion to write down its scripture as revealed, rather than just the story of its founder. It was thus able to maintain the purity of its source of inspiration.

The radical transformation of our ability to handle and communicate information, since the invention of the telegraph as the first electrical form of communication in 1844, has created new conditions for human community organization, and new pressures for the evolution of social systems, that we have still not completely assimilated. With fibre optics, information now moves at the speed of light. Electronic memories and other data-recording technologies have increased our ability to store and retrieve information by orders of magnitude at regular intervals, and no end to this progress is yet in sight. The human mind may once again become the limiting factor, since we can be saturated easily with information overload and must become increasingly selective in the information we absorb so as to make maximum use of our powers of creativity and judgement.

Such modern technologies have greatly increased the nature, range and impact of information flows and interconnections, so that today anyone can be in almost instant contact with many others all over the world, collectively through the mass media and individually by telephone, electronic mail and other communications devices. This revolution in the ways we can communicate and process information has totally transformed the potential of our social environment and of the kinds of eco that can be created. Physical separation is no longer a limitation to the richness and immediacy of communications, nor are there limits to the number of people with whom communications are possible. A single, unified global eco of the entire human race is now a physical possibility.

This fundamental change in our physical and technological world requires a complete re-examination of our institutional structures, most of which are now hopelessly out of date. The existing types of eco, that are reflected in the systems and structures of government, education, business and culture, making up our nation states and economic systems, have not yet caught up with the pace of change and the potential released by rapidly developing information and communications technologies. In particular, the physical barriers between geographic areas have fallen, shrinking the world into a village. Our technology allows us to function at a planetary scale, but our institutional evolution has not kept pace.

We should even reconsider our concepts of communities, urban areas and other geographic ecos, which, after all, evolved as they did because of the need to be in physical proximity to communicate, to exchange goods in markets, and to profit from the economic, social and cultural advantages of interchange between numbers of people. The exploding reach of our communications may now allow us to reduce the size of basic communities from megacities back to something at a more human scale.

The following sections suggest some of the ways in which the basic concepts underlying human institutions that are at the heart of our present social ecos need to be re-evaluated, whether the institutions are those of government, business, the international community or non-governmental organizations. They look first at some of the structural elements of society, and then at the dynamics of change as they relate to social structures.

Some principles of organic social organization

Starting from the basic assumption of the theory of ecos that the information held by an eco and embodied in its structure, communications channels and interlinkages is the critical element for understanding its functions and behaviour, it is possible to derive some basic principles of organization useful for restructuring society.

First, just as in biological evolution where innovation is at the individual level and communities are generated 'from the bottom up', it is neither practical nor efficient to try to plan a social eco in great detail. Creating a suitable institutional *structure* and *rules* of operation will allow communities to become self-generating and evolving to adapt to changing conditions. For instance, the hierarchy of command in an army allows the commander to set the strategy, his subordinates develop the tactics and send the units out, where the officer in charge of each unit adapts his instructions to the nature of the terrain and the resistance of the enemy. Even if some officers are lost, the survivors close ranks, fill the gaps and continue as before, because the organizational rules are clear.

The effectiveness and survival of an eco depend on its ability to *maintain its information content*, and to increase it if possible. Even if an organization works effectively in other ways in the short term, any neglect of, or damage to, its information content will threaten its long-term survival. If a country fails to keep up its educational system, for example, it may continue to function quite effectively with its existing trained manpower, but subsequent generations will not be able to take their places, and the result will be an inexorable decline. The evaluation of all social entities must look critically at this factor.

Efficiency is increased by *subdivision* and specialization, combined with increased interaction among the specialized units, as this allows information content to be increased without overloading communications channels. Socially, this may be illustrated by the principle of subsidiarity, that is delegating responsibilities or functions to the lowest level at which they can be executed satisfactorily. This applies equally to institutions and to people. One of the principles of business reorganization is to give people lower in the hierarchy more responsibility. At the same time, some mechanisms or institutions to communicate between sub-units for coordination and higher-level decision-making are required at each functional level of the system, from the family to the global community of all humanity.

The principle of *specialization* is also expressed in the acceptance of differences and the need for rank and hierarchy in functions. Some must lead and others follow. Differences in capacity and performance need to be reflected in differences in responsibility and reward. However, the differences attributed to particular functions and responsibilities do not necessarily imply differences in the rank of individual people, as is often the case in present society. The maximum effective use of the human capacities in an organization will come if individuals can be freely moved between functions, regardless of any traditional concept of rank, advancement, seniority or personal importance. This may run counter to present concepts of ego and success, but it is an ideal to be aimed for in eco-efficiency, and the resistance can be overcome through education to different expectations. The spiritual quality of humility, long out of fashion, would be useful here.

Given the autonomy and free will of individual human beings, social order and justice require the application of *rewards* and *punishments*. Rewards such as salaries, group acceptance and recognition, or individual satisfaction with meritorious deeds, help to motivate behaviour in support of the cohesion and effective functioning of social units. Punishments, ranging from the simple removal of rewards, or the fear of divine retribution, to fines, ostracism and incarceration, to remove an individual physically from society, are necessary to discourage damaging or threatening behaviour and to protect the community and its individual members from actions that could destroy it. Again, education to good citizenship should increase the sensitivity to community disapproval or minor punishments, making less necessary the more extreme forms of punishment current today.

Social organization requires reciprocal *responsibilities*. The social eco will lose cohesiveness if it does not take responsibility for needy individuals: orphans, the handicapped, the sick, the elderly, victims of catastrophes, etc. All of us risk being needy at some point in our lives, and we shall be more supportive of the sacrifices required to help others if we know we shall be helped in turn in time of need. In a larger sense, each individual should accept the responsibility to make his or her talents and potentials available to serve society and to increase the common wealth, in return for the benefits of belonging to the society. Most modern societies accept these responsibilities to some degree, but not necessarily completely and consistently. Indeed, there is a present tendency to emphasize rights but to overlook the accompanying responsibilities.

Communication of information is the key to the operation of social ecos, and all techniques to improve exchanges of information need to be fostered. The more information is exchanged, the more people understand each other's needs and develop a sense of solidarity and cooperation. Principles such as free and frank consultation thus take on special significance in community life.[1] When people learn to discuss a problem in a search for truth and in the common interest, rather than by defending a particular point of view or individual interest, then the efficiency of information sharing and decision-making increases. Such a process of consultation can be facilitated by individual values such as freedom from prejudice and respect for others, described in the previous chapter. The mechanism can be equally effective in a family, community, government or business. It represents a radical departure from most argumentation or political debate as practised today, but would be much more adaptive and supportive of effective social ecos.

Size and scale

The theory of ecos also puts in perspective the problems of scale in many institutions and structures. Western society is wedded to growth as a fundamental value, yet growth is difficult to manage because different processes and phenomena change scale in various ways. A mouse and an elephant have different shapes and physiological rates because of changes in scale; the elephant's legs are thicker to support the mass of its body, while the metabolism of the mouse is higher as it loses heat faster due to its greater surface to volume ratio. Some processes benefit from economies of scale up to a certain point, beyond which there may be rising costs or diminishing returns. Each eco will have a certain optimal size, determined by its functions and structural components. Indefinite growth in any eco is impossible and, if not controlled, will lead to collapse of the eco.

The scale that is best for different types of human interaction is very important. We can communicate intimately and in detail with a few people, but in a crowd communications become more superficial, and beyond a certain number mass delivery of information can take place but any real interaction becomes impossible. The natural approach in ecos is to break up the eco into smaller units appropriate to the scale of the activity, and then link these together in a higher-level eco, producing a nested series. The smaller ecos can preserve their own information store and maintain high interconnections internally, but communicate to the higher level only that information necessary to interrelate their activity with that of the rest of the system. This is the essence of the concept of decentralization, which is an essential counterweight to increasing size. It is the pattern underlying the organization of biological organisms into organelles, cells, tissues, organs and the body itself, and is equally appropriate to social organization.

The challenge in designing or evolving such nested series of ecos is to optimize the scale of each activity or process for both maximum efficiency and integration. We are far from understanding the optimal size for many economic activities, from agriculture through industry to energy generation, because there are many trade-offs that have to be balanced, and many costs and benefits that have not been adequately valued and considered. Giant corporations seem unable to adapt to rapidly changing markets. Giant bureaucracies stifle the societies they were meant to serve. We know little about how to interrelate multiple levels and networks of human ecos, and which functions are best implemented at particular geographic and temporal scales. Many kinds of connection have only now become technically possible. This is an area where much imagination and creativity is needed.

It is possible to imagine some approaches to the optimal sizes of human social ecos. The fragility evident in nuclear families, consisting only of parents and children, as compared to societies where more extended families are common, suggests that family units of at least three generations with some proximity of aunts, uncles, cousins, etc., may be more stable and effective in providing for the early education of children and in meeting the needs of all members. Yet many modern social practices ignore or even work against such families.

A local community, village or town is probably at an optimal size when everyone can know each other, when the whole community can gather together for special events, when the decision-makers can be in touch with all parts of the community and be aware of all its problems, and when common social services, such as schools, are at a size that balances economies of scale and the maintenance of an individual sense of belonging and participation. Similar calculations can be made for other institutions. The University of California once determined that the optimal size for a university campus was 14,000 students because at that size, among other reasons, the staff in any one department could still maintain scholarly interchange, and it was not yet necessary to begin duplicating significant library resources.

Institutional requirements

It is only possible at this point to sketch some of the general institutional requirements of a system of ecos for a peaceful and united world society. Management of a human system covering the whole planet will require decision-making mechanisms at different spatial scales. The following proposals build on the example of ecos in the natural world, with a maximum of decentralization to ensure local specificity and adaptability. As indicated previously, the ideal is for social institutions to be self-generating and organically evolving from basic sets of common values, rather than to be built to a rigid preconceived framework.

The fundamental unit of society is the individual human being.

Each person will be educated as part of the chain of information transmission from generation to generation so as to participate actively and fulfil his or her potential in society. This education will include the values appropriate to world citizenship based on unity in diversity, and to participating in the various levels of community organization.

The first social unit is the family, which is the basic educational unit for small children, transmitting language, culture and value systems from generation to generation. Priority will therefore be given to maintaining and reinforcing the family unit, and decisions on individuals will always be taken in their family context. For instance, if one of the key members of the family needs to move for professional or other reasons, measures will be taken to ensure that other family members can be equally productive in their new location.

A set of nested governmental structures will be required to carry out legislative, executive and judicial functions at different geographic scales. A local level of government is needed for each human community (village or city) and its immediate surrounding resource base. This primary level of organization, where extensive public consultation and participation are possible, will regulate most aspects of life in the community. Education, employment, health, social welfare, scientific research, environmental management and other basic functions will be rooted as much as possible at the local level. The local community will be involved in monitoring its own performance, and in using the information to manage its local economy and environment. The need for, and size of, major urban areas can also be reconsidered in the context of human psychology, economies and diseconomies of scale, and other factors.

One or more secondary, sub-national or national levels of government are necessary to balance the interests and interactions of the many communities in a region or geographic entity. Some consideration could be given to the appropriate sizes for the governmental units below the world level. At present, sovereign states range in population size from 1,000 to over 1 billion and from 0.44 to 17 million square kilometres. For many, their political boundaries do not necessarily correspond to any geographical, cultural, linguistic or ethnic reality, but reflect often arbitrary historical factors such as past wars of religion or colonization. There is no reason why a more rational future society could not adopt other boundaries and appropriate sizes for its secondary governmental units, such as major eco-regions or watersheds, that would form more logical and manageable ecos.

Any level of government will have to address the problem of managing power. The tendency of power to corrupt and to self-perpetuate is evident to a greater or lesser extent in all societies. The decline in moral and ethical values so evident today only accentuates the trend. The challenge of efficient government at any level is to design a system that provides effective leadership while maintaining sufficient checks and balances to prevent abuse of power. It is hard to find good examples of this today.

In present democratic societies, representatives of half the people try to govern while the other half do everything possible to make them fail, in the hopes of winning the next election. This is not a recipe for efficiency. Partisan politics is based on principles of division, conflict and the survival of the fittest, another expression of Darwinian values. This results in government, based on a mixture of conviction and expediency, that is vulnerable to the pressures of special interest groups with either a significant number of votes or the money to finance campaigns. The process selects individuals in search of power, with all the inherent power struggles and cults of personality that inevitably follow. Yet this is the least undesirable of the forms of government presently practised around the world.

In the context of ecos, power must no longer be seen as the advantage of one part over others.[2] This may have been appropriate at earlier stages of social evolution, but it is irrelevant, if not dangerous, to the effective functioning of an eco. Ecos require integration, not division. The emphasis must therefore be on unity, and the exercise of power and authority will need to be directed towards building confidence, support and consensus through the application of justice. This has profound implications for the workings of political structures and the way in which decision-makers should be selected, which will need to be explored as we rethink the structures of society.

World government

Our civilization is becoming increasingly vulnerable to the international power of money. National governments and their central banks are impotent, and international institutions and mechanisms inadequate, to manage the flows of capital and currencies on the world markets. Money is used by governments as an instrument of international political influence, to buy political cooperation and to impose commercial advantages. It is also increasingly being earned and used by private, business, subversive and criminal groups to advance their own aims and interests.

The only solution to the growing international scale of this problem is to bring the international economic system under effective management. Steps such as the move to a single world currency would stop exchange speculation and enforce more economic discipline on national economies. Governments will resist such changes, since they would mean a significant loss of national power, and force them to face economic realities that they have been avoiding through excessive borrowing. However, the alternative will be increasing international financial anarchy, threatening the whole economic system as we know it. A gradual shift towards effective international economic institutions seems inevitable, and a major global economic crisis could precipitate a rapid process of international institution-building, comparable to the Bretton Woods meetings that founded the World Bank and the International Monetary Fund in 1944.

The environmental problems of the planetary system are also pushing governments towards more effective international management. At present, each problem is being addressed through a separate international convention, but this cumbersome and voluntary process is proving inadequate to take and enforce difficult decisions that affect the essential interests of all countries. The major changes and sacrifices necessary to avoid or mitigate the human, economic and social impacts of global environmental damage will be accepted only if they are seen to be shared justly and universally, and it is doubtful if voluntary mechanisms can achieve this. Stronger institutional arrangements will have to be established.

There are other aspects of the functioning of the international system, including the global flow of information (communications), trade in natural resources, energy and manufactured goods, population movements, dispute settlement and peace-keeping, that require regulation and management to ensure stability and balance at the international level.

Since the current planetary system is increasingly proving to be unworkable and ungovernable, international economic, environmental and political management will ultimately require some form of world government, presumably through a strengthening and probably democratization of the institutions of the United Nations family, to create a true federation of nations with legislative, executive and judicial bodies. Yet the concept of world federation is not popular at the moment. Even the most thoughtful reviews of the international situation[3] shy away from any advocacy of a world government as unrealistic, undesirable or even dangerous. The fear of a world government is so strong that few leaders today consider it a practical possibility. National sovereignty is still a sacred principle, fiercely defended in international fora. National politicians and parliaments are afraid of any loss of their power. There is also a fear of the control a world government could exercise over planetary resources.

However, the reality is that much of the power that people are afraid to place in a world government is already in international hands beyond any kind of control, through the increasingly inter-locked network of multinational corporations, institutional investors and cartels. Obvious examples are the world capital market, the energy and petroleum industry, the agro-industry and its hold over genetic resources and agricultural chemicals, the communications/entertainment industry dominating news and culture, and the pharmaceutical industry, to name but a few. Governments claim national sovereignty over forests and minerals, and then sell them off to multinational corporations, often at unfavourable terms and with little protection for national interests. As more and more such power escapes from national governmental control, there are no international safeguards, checks and balances to limit it in the common interest.

Despite the rejection of world federation, it is not possible to escape the fact that many of today's problems come from the lack of adequate and effective mechanisms for international decision-making on issues that can only be addressed at the global level. It is therefore worth exploring some of the possible causes of this antipathy to world government, and to consider ways to respond to the legitimate concerns and objections.

One problem is the low esteem in which national governments are held today. Widespread corruption and inefficiency have discredited the idea of government in general. In such a situation, most people reason, a bigger government could only be worse. More bureaucracy would be harder to control. A world government would be too distant from the grass roots and too remote from public interests. The checks and balances, such as those between states today, or those of democratic systems that have ultimately reined in the more extreme abuses of national power, might not work. There is a risk that a world government would be just as vulnerable to special economic interests, inefficiency and corruption as national governments, but much more difficult to control.

Then there is the fear that a world government would be vulnerable to takeover by a global dictator. The memories of the attempts by Hitler, Stalin and others to dominate the world have not faded. If this occurred, there would be no possibility for a 'free world' outside to resist and eventually overthrow such a tyrant.

There is also a general lack of confidence in our ability to build a diverse community in which the interests of all members, nationalities and cultures would be safeguarded. The many observed failures to achieve this, even at the national level, do not inspire hope that a world community will be any more successful. Many fear that their cultural differences will be swallowed up by those who are more numerous or more powerful than themselves. The powerful and wealthy who dominate today's nation states similarly fear that their privileges will be taken away from them in a united and democratic world. There is no obvious mechanism to achieve a just balance between states and peoples of widely different sizes and levels of political power and economic development.

Just as various forms of national government were designed to control or compensate for less desirable human tendencies, so are we capable of planning a world federal system with safeguards against our greatest fears. Such a system will be highly decentralized (now popularly called 'subsidiarity' in Europe). Emphasis will be placed on participation, consultation and consensus, with appropriate checks and balances between the different centres of decision-making.

Institutional and structural safeguards can be designed to prevent a military or other takeover, and to avoid an uncontrollable bureaucracy. These can be built into the balance between different levels of governments, avoiding an excess concentration of power at any level. Beyond this, the best guarantee against abuse of the powers of a world government will be the high moral standards and pure intentions of those in international positions. The mechanisms to select such individuals, whether by election or appointment, will need to privilege these characteristics.

In any case, the plight of a major part of the world population is already so bad that even a worst-case scenario could hardly cause more suffering. Only a stronger global system has some chance of reducing the extreme inequalities that so divide and threaten the stability of the world today.

The other objections raised above are no different from those faced and resolved in creating other levels of government, including federations like the United States of America and the European Union. Many of these problems are also addressed by other approaches in this book. There is no one solution, but a combination of many that should be able to overcome all the objections that make a world federal government seem so undesirable today.

More organic structures

The challenge at all levels of social organization will be to create institutional arrangements that avoid becoming additional layers of inefficient bureaucracy, that reinforce the freedom, initiative and capacity in individuals and communities, that increase the flow of information and strengthen connections between all parts of the system, and that maintain flexibility and the capacity to renew themselves and change with the times. What we need are kinds of social organization that can pattern themselves after the best features of the coral reef eco and other highly evolved functional systems, features that have proven themselves over millions of years of successful evolution. Following this model, more advanced forms of human organization should be characterized by decentralized, highly diversified subsystems with widespread participation at the individual level. These are, in fact, the characteristics sought in democratic systems, whose strength is often seen to lie in the creativity, innovation and participation of individuals.

One example of what such a system might be like can be seen in the Bahá'í community, which is already operating globally on a pilot scale.[4] Its pattern of organization is rooted in the local community, where every individual can participate in regular community meetings and elections. All administration and decision-making are conducted by elected bodies of nine members, whose authority and responsibility are collective and not individual. Elections are by secret ballot from the entire membership of the community without nominations or campaigning, so that those who have demonstrated through their acts that they have the necessary qualities are favoured, rather than those who seek power. Those elected have an obligation to the community to serve on the institution. Diversity to reflect the full range of community membership in the decision-making process is so desirable that, in the case of a tie vote, the person representing a minority is automatically selected.

In this system, no individual holds any position of power or authority; this is vested only collectively in the elected institutions. Once elected, members are responsible only to their own conscience and to God, not to their electorate, which frees them from the pressures and lobbying of powerful interests common in many present democratic systems. Decisions are taken, either by consensus or, if necessary, by majority vote, after full and frank consultation in a search for the solution best encompassing all the diversity of needs and perspectives in the community. Appeals from decisions at a lower level to a higher level are always possible. Elections are annual at the local and national levels, and every five years at present at the international level. National and international elections are in stages, with the individuals in a local community or region electing delegates who, in turn, elect the national body, and the members of the national bodies serving as delegates for the election of the international body.

The function of inspirational leadership is separated from the political or administrative functions and transferred to a parallel set of appointed institutions composed of individuals selected for their personal qualities, wisdom and experience, but whose function is only to advise and encourage, not to decide, and whose only leadership role is in implementing the decisions of the administrative bodies. The system thus provides a series of checks and balances designed to draw on the strengths of the whole community and to reduce or eliminate the weaknesses of most democratic systems of today.

This new pattern of social organization already functions in a global network which makes the Bahá'í Faith the second most geographically widespread religion today after Christianity, according to the *Encyclopaedia Britannica*. It is highly decentralized and adapted to the many cultures, nations and peoples of the world, yet links them into a global system that corresponds to the increasing levels of international economic, social and cultural exchange. It is fundamentally organic and evolutionary in operation, building on the strengths of democratic systems, while compensating for their most common flaws. Its strong resemblance to natural systems suggests its adaptability to the kind of decentralized multi-level structure needed for an evolving world society, and capable of balancing human pressures with environmental requirements for sustainable development.

Business

Economic institutions also need a detailed review. There will have to be basic mechanisms of international economic management, accompanied by some powers to raise taxes to finance international activities, and probably measures of redistribution between well-endowed parts of the planet and those less well off. Within this framework, we need to define the role of business and economic ecos as specialized entities responsible for essential types of productive activities within the human system. There is an appropriate natural equivalent in the autonomous organelles within all but bacterial cells, the mitochondria and chloroplasts, that are specialized bodies with the chemical machinery to capture and release the energy needed to make cells function. The mines, factories and commerces are similar specialized ecos, often grouped into national or multinational corporations.

Present corporate structures are often models of efficiency relative to other social institutions because of the pressures of competition and the market. In an economic system where survival of the fittest is the rule, even if this is often tempered by government subsidies and protection, a business that does not reorganize as necessary to maintain its efficiency and competitiveness may find itself subject to takeovers, buy-outs or corporate raiders, if not bankruptcy and oblivion.

Unfortunately, as pointed out earlier, this efficiency is measured only in terms of production and financial return. Businesses frequently have a poor record in their use of human resources, whether it be in the turnover of managers, in labour problems and strikes, or in lay-offs of excess workers, particularly the older and higher-paid staff who have difficulty finding alternative employment. Since their basic institutional value is financial efficiency rather than justice, they pay workers whatever the market will bear, which generally means less for women than for men for equal work, and less even than a living wage if there is surplus labour desperate for any employment, unless legislation establishes a minimum wage.

For more effective and integrated ecos that share in the general responsibilities of society, we must find ways to maintain the economic efficiency, productivity and innovation of business ecos while adding a human social dimension, both for the internal benefit and long-term sustainability of the businesses themselves, and for the larger benefit of society. This will require modifying the present institutional framework and legal status, within which businesses operate, that limit their responsibility only to fiscal efficiency.

One problem, in a world of global competition, is that any major change or solution on a less than global basis will immediately handicap the businesses concerned. Already, the heavy social charges borne by businesses in industrialized countries put them at a disadvantage in international competition with countries where wages are low and social charges are limited or non-existent. Assuming that the alternative of retreating behind protectionist barriers and abandoning competition in the global market is unacceptable for other reasons, only moves to share social benefits and the results of economic activity globally on a equal basis will solve this problem. There will also need to be global anti-trust legislation to prevent excessive concentrations of economic power and control of resources in a few multinationals, which would destroy the effective operation of the market, and shift power away from governments and into the hands of a few corporate managers subject to no effective controls in the common interest.

More work is needed on the fundamental issue of how to share the wealth generated by society, particularly by its business component, so that every member benefits, without stifling initiative and the entrepreneurial spirit, and without smothering economic activities. One element of sharing is in the wages paid, including the range between the president and the lowest worker, and the total share of turnover devoted to wages. Wages are, after all, the major mechanism for redistribution of economic benefits in present society.

A related issue is how to generate and allocate the capital required for investment. Should it be accumulated within the business from internal profits not distributed as dividends, which means that it is allocated by the managers of the business according to their own criteria? Should it be distributed as dividends to investors, who are then free to reinvest, presumably looking only for the best return on their investment? Should it be collected as taxes and then distributed by the government according to its political priorities, as is done with state-owned corporations and business subsidies? Should it be accumulated as savings for retirement or security, which may leave its use in the hands of the individual saver, but more usually means that it is conferred to a bank account or pension fund, which, along with the reserves of insurance companies, are invested by a professional manager for some balance of high returns and security. These alternatives are important, because they determine whether short-term financial return is the only investment criterion, or whether other social goals, long-term interests, or other kinds of development are also considered. Any society must determine what proportion of its available capital goes to economic investments in business, or to infrastructure or other social investments, like education and welfare. Many of these choices are made today on an *ad hoc* basis, and seldom in an integrated way, even at the national level. There is no mechanism even to consider such choices at the international level where the imbalances between countries are so striking.

There is thus an intimate relationship between the way that business activity is structured and capital flows managed, and the broader concerns of the management and evolution of national and global society. Any move to go beyond a materialistic view of the world and to consider wealth in broader terms, to give people a more central place and to emphasize values of unity and justice, will require changes in the fundamental structures and roles of business in society.

Civil society

One of the phenomena of our time is the flowering of a multitude of associations and non-governmental organizations addressing almost every conceivable subject. People are no longer satisfied to wait for government to respond to the problems they see around them. They are ready to take on responsibility for themselves and to act for what they believe.[5] This is a hopeful sign of the growing motivation for change. The impact of these groups ranges from concrete actions at the grass roots of local communities to the increasing participation of non-governmental organizations in the major United Nations conferences. They may start small and weak, without many resources, but, like any eco, they can mature.

If generosity and philanthropic action are encouraged as individual virtues, then they can also find expression in group activities. The variety and diversity of such initiatives is one of their strengths. They are not constrained like governments, but have a freedom of action that should be encouraged and stimulated. For instance, in the field of humanitarian assistance, non-governmental organizations are often able to respond to disasters or crises more rapidly and effectively than governments. They are able to avoid some of the political entanglements and maintain a neutrality that allows them to reach all those in need.

These simple adaptable methods of civil society can draw attention to new issues and pioneer new approaches that can later be taken up by governments on a more permanent basis. If changing attitudes to work and careers give people more time to contribute in other ways to society, then there could be a major growth of non-governmental structures and initiatives to respond to many pressing needs. This could help to take the burden off over-stretched governments, while providing a variety of services more suited to the great diversity of human requirements.

The above sections have examined some of the structural dimensions of more organic communities and institutions. The theory of ecos also requires an analysis of the dynamics of structures and communities over time. The following sections extend this review of the restructuring required in human institutions to their permanence and sustainability.

The fallacy of permanence

An eco that is not active is dead, or at least arrested in a potential state. Movement is essential to any kind of function. A dynamic system cannot stop; standing still is not an option in a world where everything from sub-atomic particles to galaxies is in constant motion in time and space. However, the direction of movement, whether forward or backward, is important. We are on the treadmill of time, and must keep up the pace set by nature. We have no control over the speed of time. We can move ahead, fall back, or just keep up, but we can never stop.

Sustainability within ecos means net change that should be near to zero, or only slightly positive in the evolutionary sense of improvement in systems or functions. Movement in one direction or another should only be to restore the balance. Too much change in size in any direction creates an imbalance that could be fatal to the eco. This is the danger of growth for its own sake. Growth in any one material parameter cannot go on forever. A tree cannot keep growing taller, since it will reach a point where water and materials can no longer be drawn up from the roots to the crown, when the wood may be incapable of supporting its own weight, or when wind can too easily blow the tree over. If road traffic in a city keeps growing, there will eventually be so many vehicles that the streets will be filled and movement will no longer be possible. Where growth does take place, there must be constant replacement of one kind of growth by another as natural limits are reached.

While an eco must, on balance, stay within certain limits, its capital base is dynamic. Materials deteriorate; equipment depreciates; technology evolves; resources are used up. There must be constant renewal in all material things. The aim must be for balance or net improvement in the productive physical capital.

In an eco like the planet or some geographic entity, the resource base is dynamic. Renewable resources must be in balance or accumulating. The use of non-renewable resources must be balanced by recycling or by replacement by other materials.

The human resource is also dynamic, with a turnover of individuals in the constant succession of generations. Since the real human capital is the information (knowledge, skills, wisdom) contained in human beings, we must maintain the balance by the transfer and improvement of that information from generation to generation. To make real progress, each generation must know more, and make better use of its knowledge, than the one before. The human values that underlie human behaviour and that structure and stabilize social relations must also be passed intact or improved to each new generation. This is why education is crucial to human ecos.

In human society, when all of these are in balance or improving, we have an ever-advancing civilization. Thus, it is not what we are, but what we are becoming, that is important. Yet most of today's activity is in gross imbalance, in a negative direction, and we are only vaguely aware of the danger because the accounts we are using for management of our ecos are far from complete.

Unfortunately, movement can lead not only to healthy change, but also to inertia, the resistance to change. Just as the rotation of a gyroscope creates forces that hold it in position, so do many systems develop a movement that resists any change in direction. Once we are comfortable doing something, we do not want to do it any differently. Such stability can be advantageous in moderation, avoiding violent or destructive change, but it can create problems in social ecos that resist change in response to new circumstances. The larger the system, the greater the inertia, which is one reason why smaller scale is often a desirable characteristic. Ecos that resist necessary change, that become too rigid, may eventually fail catastrophically, just as species that have become too highly adapted to a narrow environmental niche easily become extinct when their environment changes.

Since change is inevitable and standing still is impossible, struggle and effort are always required. These are beneficial and bring out our good human qualities. But fear and suffering are not inevitable. A fear of change can paralyse effort, freeze creativity and inhibit the necessary risk-taking that effort requires. We must, through a transformation of values, shift the balance of motivation in society from negative and defensive to positive and dynamic. The fear of unemployment and material want should not be the basic driving force in society. We are not inherently lazy, needing the threat of the whip behind us. Real human fulfilment comes from meeting challenges and advancing in the accomplishment of our own potential, even if that advancement is not simple growth but a sustainable process of progressing in new and different ways. It is natural to be constantly replacing the old by new and higher perfections, whether in body, mind, soul or society. But it is not possible to have a goal of ease or comfort, as this would imply a slowing of effort. We can set a goal of reaching one level, but only to advance better to the next. These are values that can keep a human eco progressing.

This principle of change applies to the individual and to all the institutions of society, on both material and spiritual levels. Rising productivity, or efficient action, comes from increasing the information content and connectivity in any eco. This is the process of evolution, which is driven to ever higher levels of perfection through the law of ecodynamics described in Chapter 4. We must be constantly trying to improve our economic and human systems, just as we must protect, maintain and, if possible, improve the natural systems of the planet.

There are many time scales of change. Change in individual people is the most obvious, but each succeeding generation builds on the preceding one without exactly duplicating it. We have tended to focus on short time scales because of our preoccupation with the present. However, as we learn more about the long-term dynamics of planetary systems, we must recognize that long slow processes can also represent significant threats to our well-being if neglected.

It follows from this principle of change that no eco can or should be permanent. Every system, whether biological, mechanical or social, gradually accumulates errors, faults, inefficiencies, or even becomes unadapted as its environment changes. While simple systems may be able to maintain themselves through a constant process of renewal of defective parts, this becomes increasingly difficult in more complex systems. The ageing of the human body is an excellent example. Despite the constant repair and replacement of tissues, defects accumulate. The nervous system in particular, perhaps because of its importance in information communication, processing and storage (memory), has only very limited powers of regeneration. There is a natural tendency to sclerosis and rigidity, where change becomes difficult, and much effort is lost in struggling against the increasing inertia of the system. This is often accompanied and partly caused by an increase in size. Death and replacement are thus an inevitable part of the process of change. The cyclic rhythm of birth, maturation, reproduction, decline and death are universal characteristics of higher systems. Nature has found no other solution to this problem.

Bureaucracy: the final solution

The same principles apply to all human ecos and social structures. As human institutions become bureaucratic, rigid and inefficient, they need to be renewed or replaced. In the past, war and revolution have been the principal instruments for such institutional renewal. History is largely a description of the rise and fall of rulers and governments, usually through violence, which had the incidental effect of permitting institutional replacement and renewal. In the modern world, we should ask if war and revolution are not unnecessarily painful and uncivilized processes. Just as modern medicine has largely replaced blood-letting, amputation and surgery without anaesthetic, so we must find better approaches to social and institutional healing and rejuvenation.

It should be possible to plan for the reconstruction or phasing out and replacement of over-age institutions. In simple organizations run by a single leader, changing the leader may be sufficient, but in larger institutions that have grown beyond the control of any single person, a more radical approach is needed to clear away the accumulated weight of bureaucracy. We must recognize that everything moves in cycles, and there are limits to the duration of all corporations, governmental structures, international agencies, religions and other social systems when they reach a point of diminishing returns. This may mean testing the capacity of institutions for resilience and change, planning for their periodic evaluation and renewal, or even fixing a limit or lifespan at their creation. This is the only solution to the strangle-hold of bureaucracy and the inertia of large systems. A process of institutional death, rebirth and renewal needs to be accepted and built into our society. The young and energetic must break off and build anew, while the old must consciously evolve, or fade away and die a natural death.

This life-cycle concept of ecos should apply everywhere in society, at appropriate time scales. We must find the best time periods for institutional cycles, or develop means of diagnosing the symptoms of institutional sclerosis to know when to close out and replace old, unadapted structures, such as government ministries, legal codes and tax systems. Each type of institution may have its own appropriate lifespan. Religions as basic value systems for society seem to follow cycles of renewal of about a thousand years, although the man-made institutions, hierarchies and rituals that have been added to them may need change at more frequent intervals. For governmental bureaucracies, pragmatic observations suggest that a life cycle of about forty years may be appropriate. The two most dynamic nations of the last half century, Germany and Japan, were able to renew all their economic, social, legal and governmental structures and infrastructure after World War II, and it seems to have taken about forty years for them to reach a point of rigidity and conservatism comparable to other nations. The need for renewal in the United Nations was also accepted after it passed 40 years. It may be necessary to develop some tests for institutional dynamism and the capacity for self-renewal, in order to determine which institutions are beyond saving, so that they can be shut down and replaced. Modern governmental bodies and civil services are particularly resistant to change because they have been designed with extreme job security and multiple safeguards to protect them from manipulation, corruption and frequent political changes at the top. The pressure for privatization of government services, now popular in some countries, reflects the difficulty of changing the public sector and the assumption that private entities can be more dynamic and efficient.

Corporate businesses often suffer from similar institutional sclerosis, but the pressures of competition usually do not allow them to remain indefinitely as immobile as government structures. They may be forced to undertake a major reorganization into smaller and more efficient units, be swallowed up and digested in a takeover, be dismantled and sold off by corporate raiders, or simply wither away and disappear like Pan American World Airways.

Closing out an old institution is the hardest part, because there are always strong vested interests among employees and clients in maintaining the *status quo*. People are naturally afraid of losing their jobs and status, and of facing the uncertainty of change. Effective institutional renewal requires special attention to its human dimension. For excess government bureaucracies, it might be cheaper to pension off all the staff, regardless of age, rather than to keep them in jobs where they only make unnecessary work for others in the system, but more constructive approaches to reusing the available human talent would be desirable.

One constraint is the natural 40–50-year cycle of individual working lives, which may be longer than the necessary cycling of institutional change. In those countries and fields where people are trained in their youth for one occupation and expect to remain and progress in that occupation until retirement, there will be resistance to all change at time scales shorter than a full career. However, the new concepts of human resources management, discussed in the previous chapter, can facilitate such change. If it is no longer necessary for individuals to hold on to job security, but on the contrary they are encouraged to search for new challenges in a society that accepts and supports occupational change, then the *status quo* becomes less important. A social 'safety net' to prevent extreme deprivation and ensure that dependents do not suffer from individual failure will also help to eliminate the fear of risk-taking. As with the experience of all children, failure is normal, uncomfortable and negative, but there must be an encouragement to rise above the set-back and to try again, to rebuild confidence. The same should apply throughout individual careers and lifetimes. This is part of the necessary exploring and fulfilling of each person's potential.

It is thus such a dynamic approach to the use of human capital that makes complete institutional life cycles possible, allowing for the necessary change and renewal as a natural and normal process of social evolution.

How might such an approach work in practice? There is more renewal already in the private sector, because competition does not allow inefficiency to accumulate for long without it becoming apparent in business performance. The problem is more serious in government, where new bodies are often created because of the difficulty in reforming or replacing the old ones. There, it may be necessary to put a statutory limit on governmental structures at their creation, after which they would be subjected to tests of flexibility, efficiency and viability, and if necessary dissolved and new structures put in their place, assuming that their functions were still necessary. Legislators would have to build such provisions into the laws organizing government. For essential services such as tax collecting, there could be some transition period, during which critical information and experience could be transmitted to the new body, and new approaches would have time to be tested. Whenever possible, institutional renewal should aim to reduce in size, to simplify and decentralize, breaking large ecos into smaller and more efficient ones closer to those they are serving. Different processes of renewal and replacement would have to be developed for each institutional situation to ensure the process led to efficiency and improvement, and not just to disruption.

In some circumstances, a preventive approach to developing bureaucracy may be possible as part of an institutional design. Keeping organizations or units small can help, as inertia increases with size. Challenging and encouraging them to evolve and adapt, for instance through competition, is another option. Staff rotations may be appropriate in some cases to prevent entrenchment and to provide new opportunities. A regular process of complete renewal or re-election of the members of small institutions (of, say, less than twenty people), with no priority or advantage for incumbents, might be sufficient to maintain dynamism. It is in larger bodies, where institutional inertia escapes from individual control, that more drastic remedies may be the only solution.

Notes

1. For a good description of methods of consultation, see Kolstoe (1985).
2. Bahá'í International Community (1995), VI.
3. Gore (1992); Daly and Cobb (1994); Commission on Global Governance(1995).
4. Dahl (1994a).
5. Ekins (1992) gives one encouraging listing.

CHAPTER 9

Visions of an eco-civilization

The latest scientific evidence of the process of biological evolution suggests that it is not necessarily a smooth gradual process. The pressures for change build up on a well-established and stable system until finally something gives, and the system is overthrown by rapid changes, perhaps building on important advances made during the period of stability, leading to a new and more advanced system. The first mammals evolved as quite insignificant small animals during the age of the dinosaurs, but with the collapse of that reptile-dominated period, the mammals were able to fan out and evolve rapidly into a new set of dominant species.

Human social evolution seems to follow a similar pattern, with bursts of creative social organization and the blossoming of a civilization with a particular set of institutions and other social ecos, followed by relative stability and then decline, preparing the way for the next advance. The depressing litany of problems reviewed in Chapters 2 and 3 would not inspire much hope for the future, if it were not for the increasing evidence that we are passing through one of those critical evolutionary transitions. The technological transformation of our physical environment has precipitated the decline and imminent collapse of the institutions, patterns of human relationships and ways of thinking adapted to what might be described as humanity's childhood and adolescence, while we are simultaneously experiencing the birth-pangs of a new global human system, initiating the age of humanity's adulthood, based on the unity of the human race that is only now possible.

What this means is that we must question, re-examine and transform every aspect of our society. We must rethink our social and economic concepts and assumptions, and reshape every institution at every level of society. We have a unique opportunity, challenge and responsibility to design, consciously and systematically, our own future.[1] This is not just another responsibility for governments, which are themselves caught in the turmoil of change, but for all people, and it must be done for the benefit of the whole human race. This book aims to help stimulate that process.

The fear of change

Social change has always been a difficult and painful process, as the American, French, Russian and Chinese revolutions have demonstrated, to cite a few examples. People are naturally afraid of abandoning their existing institutions and ways of thinking for something new and different, and there are always vested interests in preserving the *status quo*. Yet a glance at history shows how much the fundamental institutions of all societies have had to change over time. In a world where the environment and technology are evolving at increasing speed, institutional change must inevitably follow. What we must try to avoid is allowing the pressures to build up to the breaking point where only a violent revolution is possible.

The rise of anarchy, chaos, terrorism and genocide in our own time does not inspire confidence in our ability to manage change. We tend to cling to the sinking ship, or even to deny that it is sinking at all. Yet in times of danger or crisis, calm and rationality have great survivor value. Scuba divers, for instance, must learn never to panic even in the most dire conditions, but to reflect on the alternative solutions to their problem and rely on their buddies, even while at great depth and on their last breath; such calm has often made the difference between death and survival. We need the same approach collectively as we examine our social predicament.

To overcome, or at least temper, the fear of change, we should recognize that we do not need to leap blindly into the void. This means starting with a clear vision of where we want to go even if we are not always certain just how to get there. One of the aims of this book is to stimulate the process of defining that vision, and to enlarge the circle of people thinking creatively about our future. We also need confidence in the processes at work, and for this the theory of ecos shows that it is natural for all organisms, including social organisms, to evolve. There are sufficient models in nature, of the proven effectiveness of complex systems like ours, for us to imitate their features with some hope of success. We can be reasonably optimistic about the inherent resilience and creativity in human society, and about the ability of democratic consultative institutions with adequate checks and balances to guide the process. The main challenge is to establish a foundation of shared values sufficiently strong to ensure cohesiveness and to counteract the negative and destructive tendencies in present-day society.

As we examine what will be required to plan our future, it should be apparent from the preceding chapters that all the dimensions of human ecos are interrelated, and that change in each element is necessary for and supports the others. Renewed values are necessary to motivate new behaviour in people. New institutional approaches will increase responsiveness and efficiency, but only if reinforced with new patterns of human behaviour. New economic mechanisms will allow society to develop its productive potential in more effective and complete ways. Clearly, it is going to be difficult to get all these levels of change to move forward in synchrony, so that they are self-reinforcing. We are feeling our way along towards a new society, and shall need to experiment on a small scale, and in particularly propitious situations, until we have established some confidence in the directions we are taking. The real danger is in the immobilism that could come from the fear of any change, or the sense of helplessness at the complexity of the situations we face.

The organic framework of ecos

The theory of ecos provides a unifying framework explaining the workings of all functional systems, including our own, and bringing together the economic, environmental, social and even spiritual dimensions of our society. It shows the importance of achieving and maintaining a balance in all material inputs to, and outputs from, an eco. In particular, it demonstrates the importance of the information held within a system and determining its structure and the extent of its connectivity and integration, as well as the way the flow of energy driving an eco can assist in building its information content. This information is in fact the true wealth of all ecos, including those of human society. Redefining the most important wealth as that of information can help us to break out of the present materialistic world-view, which dominates so much current thinking, and to consider some visions of the future.

It may help to summarize some of the implications of the analyses in the preceding chapters for individuals, communities, governments, and the economic system, as they all contribute to the framework of a new, more organic society.[2]

Human ecos, whether individual or social, are ultimately organized, driven and perpetuated by information, represented at the highest level by the processes of our mind and the values that guide our individual and social development. Thus the essence of human nature is not our physical body and its material needs, but our consciousness. We are essentially what has traditionally been called spiritual beings. This can lead us to define the purpose of life, and thus of development, as being to fulfil our human potential, which, being rooted in consciousness, is basically an information potential. Guided by our values, we acquire material and spiritual knowledge, add to it from our own experience, and pass it on to succeeding generations. Even the work we do has a spiritual dimension, through the qualities acquired by being of service to society. In the context of ecos, our highest aim becomes to produce wealth not for ourselves, but for all humankind. Our new environment, leading to a unified world society, requires new values and a transformation of our attitudes and relationships. Cooperation and a sense of duty will replace conflict and self-centredness. Love, forgiveness, generosity, trust, discipline, sacrifice and contentment are qualities that will facilitate human interactions in social ecos, and the productivity of the real wealth that is knowledge, science and culture. We need not wait for anyone else, but should start to act now, in whatever way we can, to change ourselves and the world around us. Many people are already doing so.

The transformation of social institutions starts with the family and extends to communities at all levels. Our collective motivation will increasingly be rooted in a desire for social justice, which requires a reduction in the extremes of wealth and poverty in the world. The community values necessary are unity in diversity, equality, collaboration, conciliation, and a sense of our collective responsibility for the welfare of every human being. The basic operating principles will be participation and consultation. We must be confident in the collective capacity of all peoples to consider the issues and to decide and plan for themselves. Already, there are hopeful signs that many concerned people are not waiting for governments, but are beginning to act for change through various movements and associations.

The challenge for governments at all levels is to develop a new concept of power, not as an advantage over others in the competition for domination, but as partners in building the necessary unity in the world, based on a sense of global responsibility. Governments need to cultivate a new attitude, seeking the confidence, respect and support of their citizens, whom they should consult openly. Their central purpose should be to maintain unity in their country or community. A democratic system is the most desirable for this, but with refined electoral procedures. A new global level of government is required through a federation of nations, to establish the laws and institutions necessary to protect the environment and development needs of all people.

A central theme of this book has been the inadequacy of economics as presently understood and managed to resolve many fundamental problems of today, or even to provide adequate measures of what is generally called development. The over-reliance of many leaders on an essentially economic and thus materialistic view of society has blinded them to many critical flaws and imbalances in today's system of nation states. We use detailed economic statistics and accounting systems for monetary flows and financial debt. However, systems to account for the increasing burden of environmental and natural resource debt are only beginning to be put in place, and the means to account for the massive social debt represented by poverty and the general wastage of human resources have yet to be designed. To resolve these problems, new economic models are required, based not on a materialistic view of society and an impersonal market mechanism, but incorporating principles such as unity and justice. Their orientation should be altruistic rather than self-seeking, aimed to favour human relationships, including the family and community. The structures of business should be adapted accordingly.

The knowledge society

A society reoriented from money to knowledge as the central focus of development will be able to build on the enormous progress our civilization has made. We have, in fact, built information tools that are as good at processing and distributing knowledge, the new currency of civilization, as they are at accounting for money. The information required is so varied that it would be impossible to try to define it here. It ranges from the scientific information about our environment that may tell us if it will rain or shine tomorrow, through statistics on the number of people with paid employment or the rules that regulate air traffic flow, to the music that expresses our most exalted emotions. It includes everything written in books and the largely unconscious rules that govern how we greet a stranger. It varies with the individual, nation, language and culture. Its diversity is its richness, and the secret of its preservation and development lies in the effectiveness with which it is used, stored and communicated.

Technology has today enabled us to break through most of the barriers to information storage and communications capacity. We can now collect and process data at scales and speeds that were previously unimaginable, and improvements continue at a rapid pace. We have thus acquired the potential to make almost any information tools we want. This presents us with a new challenge, set by our own human information capacity. We can be flooded and drowned by information that is highly variable in its value and utility. In fact, media like television can saturate our senses and play on the emotions to the point that the brain has no time for deep reflection. We may even use information as an escape from reality and a distraction from difficult problems or situations in life that we do not know how to face.

The flood of data and information available today requires techniques to sift, select, rank and evaluate it. Controlled information flow is one of the characteristics of successful ecos, allowing just the necessary communications and storage without wasting resources on excess capacity. Ecos are often subdivided or nested in order to achieve the most economical information flows and linkages.

Information can be ranked from raw data and observations, as collected for instance from scientific instruments, up a scale of added value and judgement towards knowledge and wisdom. The proportion of objective scientific data diminishes as the more subjective but perhaps more socially useful component increases. The artistic equivalent would be a scale from raw musical notes or colours to a completed symphonic work or painting. As the flow of data and information increases, so must our efficiency and effectiveness in transforming it into useful knowledge, and this is a particular weakness in information systems as they exist today. Computerized tools are more useful at the lower end of the scale, but judgements and evaluations are more difficult to programme into a computer. The choice of what information is really important involves both scientific and ethical components, combining perceptions of the objective reality and subjective evaluations. The task is easier if there is already a shared set of basic values, and one challenge for future society is to identify and reinforce the common elements in widely shared human values.

We can make expert systems that mimic an expert's own analytical processes and include the expert's own value judgements. Such systems facilitate repetitive analyses where standard criteria can be applied, but will machines ever be able to match the full range of human diversity and creativity? And even if they could, would this be desirable? The information revolution should liberate rather than replace the human mind by increasing access to information, sifting out extraneous material, and facilitating assimilation. Above all, it is the possibility of more efficient communication around the world that is opening an unimaginable potential for new kinds and scales of human ecos by increasing the scale and speed of human interchange.

If we assume that people should remain central to information processing, even if they are helped by ever-more-sophisticated tools, then we must design supportive information systems for decision-making, creation and education. Such systems will increase access to all the necessary facts and information. They can include the means to analyse and integrate that information, to project trends and to examine the implications of alternative choices. We also need to develop better human processing and decision-making, not just by increasing the intellectual powers of individuals (who are inherently limited and culture-centred), but also through collective groups and consultative processes, where the weaknesses and blind spots of each individual can be cancelled out and personal strengths can become additive. At present, many decision-makers do not even know how to use information in any organized way; they simply respond to the pressures around them, integrating them with political judgement. In our increasingly complex world, the challenges of sustainable development call for more systematic and coherent use of information in policy development and decision-making.

The ultimate goal should not be an information society, much discussed today, with its focus on hardware, software and networking. These are only tools. We should be aiming for a knowledge society, in which the information flowing in and between many levels of ecos is incorporated in people as useful knowledge and expressed in the rich functioning of many ecos. The combination of that knowledge and the renewed values underlying society will produce wisdom and an advancing civilization.

Some characteristics of future society

While it is impossible to predict the future, there are implications of the theory of ecos that can suggest some of the possible characteristics of the more organic world society to come.[3]

A central goal of the management of the global eco will be long-term sustainability. It is possible to envisage a global civilization on this planet extending for at least half a million years. This is a hundred times all of recorded history, during which time many civilizations have risen and fallen, often because of unsustainable use of their resources. This means that at a planetary scale our material society must achieve something approaching a steady state as it reaches global limits. The only material growth permitted will come from increases in the efficiency of the system. Growth in the sense of exploiting untapped resources and opening new markets, as we know it today, will rarely be possible, and development will have to be qualitative rather than quantitative. The real continuing growth will be in information, the rich activities that will flourish in the sciences, medicine, art and culture, and in services building interpersonal and community relations, supported by educational processes to ensure the continuing transmission and use of that information and the maintenance of a close-knit social fabric.

We are far from achieving this today, with both our population growth and our consumption of resources running out of control. The longer we wait to master these trends, the more we are apt to damage the carrying capacity of the Earth, lowering the standard of living ultimately attainable, or the size of a sustainable world community, or both. On the other hand, it is impossible to predict today what the ultimate capacity of this planet for human society may be, as this will depend on our technology and efficiency, as well as on the type of life-style and level of per-capita resource consumption we select. The population problem today is much more one of the speed of change rather than the absolute numbers. We simply cannot create the wealth and spread the information necessary to provide the rapidly swelling numbers of people with education, employment or the resources from which they can make their own living.

Agriculture will have to provide the productive basis for any future civilization, since the rapid exhaustion of the non-renewable resources by our own age will leave renewable resources as the principal future source of raw materials. However, future agriculture will be very different from that we know today, which is based primarily on unstable, chemical-intensive monocultures. With advances in biotechnology and improvements in ecosystem science, it should be possible to design complex, integrated and balanced multi-species systems, of which humanity is an integral part, which can simultaneously maintain the life-support systems of the planet, provide the food and raw materials needed for society, absorb and recycle our waste products, and create an aesthetically pleasing living environment. We should be able to engineer ecosystems the way we engineer bridges today, producing delightful urban forests and surroundings resembling the mythical Garden of Eden. Within such systems, all manufactured materials will be carefully managed through their whole life cycle to eliminate the effects of pollution and to preserve scarce non-renewable resources.

As all available sources of energy are harnessed to power the future civilization, renewable energy sources will become predominant, while fossil fuels will be phased out because of their unacceptable environmental impact, particularly on the atmosphere and climate. Energy will be the key factor limiting the standard of living that the future world will be able to provide, but great increases in energy efficiency will be possible.

Another key principle for the management of the future global eco is moderation. As Bahá'u'lláh warned over a hundred years ago, material civilization carried to excess would be as great a source of evil as it had been of good when kept within the restraints of moderation.[4] It is now apparent that the atmosphere cannot tolerate some of our chemical products, as shown by the damage to the ozone layer. The increase in greenhouse gases threatens to disturb the planet's thermal stability. Many toxic and persistent chemicals are building up in the environment, with a potential threat to human health and other life. Our rush for development is destroying rich agricultural areas, forests, soils, fisheries and other productive renewable resources, not to mention the genetic resources and biological diversity that contribute to global stability and could be extremely valuable in the future as information resources for a biotechnological civilization. We shall therefore need to be more selective in the kinds of technology we develop and apply widely, accepting a simpler life-style in some ways while increasing technology and sophistication in others, particularly those concerned with information communications, storage and use. The aim will be a better balance between the physical, social, intellectual and spiritual dimensions of life.

A re-emphasis on the knowledge, information content and integration of society as the true wealth will help in this direction. Information in itself does not have environmental impact, and can probably be accumulated without limit. The possibilities to enrich our lives through science, education, music, art, drama and literature are endless. This is one market that will never be saturated. It is also scientific and technical information that can help to increase our efficiency of energy and material use. Information can assist us to achieve a more environmentally sound and sustainable civilization, raising our quality of life while bringing the material systems that support us back into balance with planetary limits.

The first steps

There is little point in laying out plans for the future if we have no idea how to implement them. The following suggestions include actions which both governments and individuals can take as first steps towards a brighter future. They obviously require more elaboration than is possible here, but should at least provide an initial agenda for consideration.

All members of society, and particularly its leaders, must accept the essential principle of the oneness of humankind and the associated ideal of world citizenship. This is the fundamental concept upon which the necessary global eco can be established. It should be the subject of educational campaigns to reach the public, through programmes in the schools and using the mass media. This principle and its associated spiritual value, justice, must be vigorously encouraged to counteract the wave of racial, tribal, sectarian and chauvinistic violence now sweeping the world and tearing countries and societies apart. We must not stand by idly while these social diseases are eating into the vitals of society, but must make every effort to apply a counteracting remedy.

People everywhere should become involved in planning their future and formulating common goals within the context of the shared global responsibility implied by the oneness of humanity. Consultation is the operating principle of justice, so the institutions of society and all plans and projects for development should be rebuilt on this foundation.

The focus of all efforts should be on essential social and economic priorities, particularly the elimination of poverty and the establishment of universal standards and benefits for human life on this planet. This will mean reversing the trends in the accumulation of all kinds of debt, including endemic poverty and underdevelopment, excessive population growth, accumulating pollution and unsustainable resource consumption. Then there will have to be an enormous effort to pay off the backlog of human, environmental and financial debts that our profligate age has accumulated.

We must accelerate the universal spread of scientific and techno-logical activities to all nations and people. Everyone should have access to knowledge, and be educated to make the best use of it. The scientific approach, including a dedication to truth, and thinking in terms of process, will help all societies to progress. At the same time, a dialogue should be maintained with religion, so that the material discoveries of science can be weighed with moral principle and implemented through spiritual commitment.

We must also cultivate a sense of responsibility and trusteeship for the environment, and learn to live within its limits. This will require mechanisms for global decision-making for those processes and resources that can only be addressed at the global level.

As we launch these actions, we need, at the same time, to be laying the foundations for new social and economic systems based on an integrated view of global society. In this we can draw inspira-tion from those natural and organic systems that have demonstrated their value over millions of years of evolution, whose strengths can be analysed with the theory of ecos as shown in Chapter 5. This will mean moving away from a money-centred system, designed by and for those who have money, towards a more balanced accounting and management system, including human resources, natural re-sources and life-support systems, capital and monetary resources, the built resources of the human habitat and infrastructure, and information resources. Using measures of all these components, and allowing for those dimensions that can never be measured and compared, we can expect to find a very different weighting and valuation of societies from what we are accustomed to today, because the diverse civilizations and communities have 'developed' in very different ways. Some of the so-called developed countries may prove to be quite backward in human resources utilization and natural resources management, for example, while some materially simpler societies may rate quite highly in these areas.

In this way, ecology and economy will become complementary approaches and tools for the study and management of the many ecos making up society. Their unity will provide a coherent frame-work for the material and scientific aspects of civilization, needing only to be brought into harmony with the human and spiritual dimensions of life for a fully rounded approach to our future.

Placing people and their capacity to store, manipulate and use knowledge and information at the heart of our concerns is the key to the whole process. If the highest social value is placed on the development of all the available human potential in the service of our collective advancement, then many of the present disfunctions in society will vanish. A new set of universal values will provide the foundation for the necessary changes in human behaviour, motivating everyone to contribute constructively to society. Education will become the critical process for the perpetuation and advancement of all scales of human ecos from the family and local community to the global society.

That society will need to be organized and structured in new ways, adapted to higher levels of integration. This will require both central institutions at the world level to provide global coordination and balance, in what would be some form of federated world government, and a nested series of subsidiary ecos providing for a decentralized and diverse set of governmental and productive institutions down to the local level. The larger scales of organization will need to include safeguards against the creeping dangers of over-centralization and bureaucracy, while ensuring the application of the principle of justice necessary to regulate the affairs of nations and peoples. A continuing process of change and renewal will need to become as much a normal part of social structures as it is of natural systems.

The essential concept that must become central to our world-view is the fact that this planet is, at its largest scale, a single eco, a global human community linked to and dependent on the Earth's natural systems. At this level, the oneness of humanity and the oneness of nature come together. The global eco is bound by the same rules as any eco, which means that all the accounts within the eco must be in balance. Many of our problems stem from the fact that we have ignored the existence of a planetary eco and have not worried about balances at the global level.

Since the planet is, to all intents and purposes, a closed system, any material growth or development in one area that exceeds the local resource capacity implies losses and transfers out of other areas, unless compensated by equitable exchanges. Unequal transfers, especially from the poor to the rich, are contrary to the principle of justice. It is often convenient for those who are benefiting from the gains to forget or ignore this fact, just as the wealthy may try not to notice that their advantage may ultimately be related to the disadvantage of others. For example, in any system of global trade, exports and imports must ultimately balance. Clearly, the flows of goods and money that drive commerce can be differentiated and to some extent substituted, but they must be compensating if there is not to be an accumulation of wealth and well-being in some places and of poverty and debt in others.

In any eco, the creation of new wealth, whether by sustainable increases in the efficiency of production of renewable resources, or by the value added from increased capital and information, can benefit the producing areas and raise the general level of wealth to the extent that they exceed the consumption of resources, the depreciation of capital and the loss of information. The balancing transfers to adjust for differences in capacities and resource endowments across the planet can be earned, or be based on planned redistribution or subsidy, but they must ultimately take place if differences are not to become more and more extreme. Accompanying such transfers with a universal ethic of service and an obligation to work will ensure that everyone carries an appropriate share of responsibility. A recognition of this requirement for balance at the global level will alter the rules of exchanges between nations and regions. It will be necessary to give more in order to get more. World unity requires the application of justice in the use and distribution of resources in order to assure long-term stability of any kind.

While it would be nice to know precisely where we are going, we must recognize that we cannot plan our future in detail. Nature does not do so, and any thought on our part that this is possible is a fallacy generated by excessive pride in the human intellect. We need to leave room for surprises in nature and imagination and creativity in humanity. In our designs for the future, we must set our goals, as a ship's captain will set a destination and chart a course, and use these as points of reference as we advance, but not fall into the error of detailed central planning. The organic pattern of development of any eco is to set the ground rules (in this case the basic values and principles of human interaction) and then allow the system and the individuals who compose it the freedom to develop with all their initiative, diversity, creativity and adaptability. It is thus critically important to get the rules right, based on values that are universally accepted as fundamental to human progress and fulfilment.

The multiple levels of ecos that make up the social structure must be linked in ways that maximize the information flow and connectivity between them to reduce barriers to their evolution. We then must design systems of monitoring the information flow that relate to those basic values, so that our individual and group efforts to manage our development are guided by feedback on the most critical factors in our economic and social evolution. This monitoring must clearly be centred on universal human welfare and betterment, which must be the ultimate measure of sustainable development.

All this may seem idealistic and even utopian, but it is not beyond our reach. We may never be able to escape the cycles of civilization, but we can take hope from the fact that the collapse of an old order is a necessary prelude to its replacement by a new and better system. Our perspective is too short to appreciate just where we are in the cycle, but the evidence suggests that we are passing through the darkest point in the transition, where the speed of disintegration is beginning to reinforce the still scattered but growing efforts at integration and reconstruction. Fortunately, the new information technologies have spread knowledge so widely that we can probably avoid the extended dark ages of previous cycles of civilization. While the transition will be difficult, the future is full of hope.

The human capacity to acquire and use knowledge is far above anything that has been experienced to date. The acceptance of the essential unity of humanity within a framework of universally agreed values will create the potential for the next new step forward in our social and spiritual evolution. As our ability to assimilate knowledge grows, so will our potential to synthesize and combine that knowledge in creative new ways, opening up unimaginable possibilities for the human spirit. Bringing our natural, material and human dimensions into balance through rational management of our global eco will thus lay the foundations for the flowering of a world-wide civilization.

Notes

1. Bahá'í International Community (1995).
2. Some of the concepts in this section are developed further in Bahá'í International Community (1995).
3. Some of these ideas have also been developed in Dahl (1990).
4. Bahá'u'lláh (1939) *Gleanings*, CLXIII, pp. 342–3.

Selected bibliography

'Abdu'l-Bahá (1945) *Foundations of World Unity*, compiled from addresses and tablets of 'Abdu'l-Bahá, Bahá'í Publishing Trust, Wilmette, Illinois.

'Abdu'l-Bahá (1957) *The Secret of Divine Civilization*, translated from the original Persian text by Marzieh Gail, Bahá'í Publishing Trust, Wilmette, Illinois.

Artigiani, Robert (1993) 'Building a Global Society: Progress and Procedures', pp. 30–42, in Suheil Bushrui, Iraj Ayman and Ervin Laszlo (eds), *Transition to a Global Society*, Oneworld Publications, Oxford.

Bahá'í International Community (1995) *The Prosperity of Humankind*, Bahá'í World Centre, Haifa, Israel.

Bahá'u'lláh (1939) *Gleanings from the Writings of Bahá'u'lláh*, translated by Shoghi Effendi, Bahá'í Publishing Trust, Wilmette, Illinois (and various subsequent editions).

Bahá'u'lláh (1954) *The Hidden Words of Bahá'u'lláh*, translated by Shoghi Effendi, revised edition, Bahá'í Publishing Committee, Wilmette, Illinois (and other international editions).

Bahá'u'lláh (1992) *The Kitáb-i-Aqdas: The Most Holy Book*, Bahá'í World Centre, Haifa, Israel.

Biffi, Franco (1989) *The 'Social Gospel' of Pope John Paul II: a Guide to the Encyclicals on Human Work and the Authentic Development of Peoples*, Pontifical Lateran University, Rome.

Bushrui, Suheil, Iraj Ayman and Ervin Laszlo (eds) (1993) *Transition to a Global Society*, Oneworld Publications, Oxford.

Capra, Fritjof (1981) *The Turning Point: Science, Society and the Rising Culture*, Simon & Schuster, New York.

Capra, Fritjof (1989) *Uncommon Wisdom: Conversations with Remarkable People*, Flamingo (HarperCollins), London.

Commission on Global Governance (1995) *Our Global Neighborhood*, Oxford University Press, Oxford.

Costanza, Robert (ed.) (1991) *Ecological Economics: The Science and Management of Sustainability*, Columbia University Press, New York.

Dahl, Arthur L. (1971) 'Development, Form and Environment in the Brown Alga *Zonaria farlowii* (Dictyotales)', *Botanica Marina* 14: 76–112.

Dahl, Arthur L. (1985) *Traditional Environmental Management in New Caledonia: A Review of Existing Knowledge*, South Pacific Regional Environment Programme, Topic Review 18, South Pacific Commission, Nouméa, New

Caledonia. Reprinted with modifications as 'Traditional environmental knowledge and resource management in New Caledonia', in R.E. Johannes (ed.) (1989), *Traditional Ecological Knowledge: A Collection of Essays*, International Union for the Conservation of Nature and Natural Resources, Gland and Cambridge.

Dahl, Arthur Lyon (1990) *Unless and Until: A Bahá'í Focus on the Environment*, Bahá'í Publishing Trust, London.

Dahl, Arthur L. (1994a) 'Ecological Models of Social Organization: A Bahá'í Perspective', pp. 15–17, in Irena Hanouskova, Miloslav Lapka and Eva Cudlinova (eds), *Ecology and Democracy: The Challenge of the 21st Century*, Proceedings of the First International Conference, Ceske Budejovice, 6–9 September 1994, full abstracts, Institute of Landscape Ecology, ASCR, Ceske Budejovice, Czech Republic.

Dahl, Arthur L. (1994b) 'Global Sustainability and Its Implications for Trade', in Papers presented at the GATT Symposium on Trade, Environment and Sustainable Development, *GATT Trade and Environment Bulletin* 9: 87–9.

Dahl, A.L., B.C. Patton, S.V. Smith and J.C. Zieman, Jr. (eds) (1974) 'A preliminary coral reef ecosystem model', *Atoll Research Bulletin* 172: 7–36.

Daly, Herman E. (1991) 'Elements of Environmental Macroeconomics', pp. 32–46, in Robert Costanza (ed.), *Ecological Economics: The Science and Management of Sustainability*, Columbia University Press, New York.

Daly, Herman E. and John B. Cobb, Jr (1989, 1994) *For the Common Good: Redirecting the Economy Toward Community, the Environment, and a Sustainable Future*, second edition, updated and expanded (1994), Beacon Press, Boston, Massachusetts.

Douthwaite, R. (1992) *The Growth Illusion: How Economic Growth Has Enriched the Few, Impoverished the Many, and Endangered the Planet*, Resurgence Books, England. [Not seen.]

Duchrow, Ulrich (1987) *Global Economy: A Confessional Issue for the Churches?*, WCC Publications, Geneva. [Not seen.]

Ekins, Paul (ed.) (1986) *The Living Economy: A New Economics in the Making*, Routledge and Kegan Paul, London and New York.

Ekins, Paul (1992) *A New World Order: Grassroots Movements for Global Change*, Routledge, London and New York.

Fondation pour le Progrès de l'Homme and Groupe de Vézelay (1993) *Plateforme pour un Monde Responsable et Solidaire*, Fondation pour le Progres de l'Homme, Paris.

Gaillard, Jean-Michel (1989) *Jules Ferry*, Fayard, Paris.

Georgescu-Roegen, Nicolas (1979) *Demain la décroissance: entropie, écologie, économie*, Editions Pierre-Marcel Favre, Paris and Lausanne.

Gore, Al (1992) *Earth in the Balance: Ecology and the Human Spirit*, Houghton Mifflin Company, Boston, New York, London.

Hardin, Garrett (1991) 'Paramount Positions in Ecological Economics', pp. 47–57, in Robert Costanza (ed.), *Ecological Economics: The Science and Management of Sustainability*, Columbia University Press, New York.

Henderson, Hazel (1988) *The Politics of the Solar Age: Alternatives to Economics*, revised edition, Knowledge Systems Inc., Indianapolis, Indiana.

Koestler, Arthur (1967) *The Ghost in the Machine*, Hutchinson, London. [Not seen.]

Kolstoe, John E. (1985) *Consultation: A Universal Lamp of Guidance*, George Ronald, Oxford.

Lamb, Robert (1993) 'Designs on life', *New Scientist*, 30 October 1993, pp. 37–40.

Laszlo, Ervin (1989) *The Inner Limits of Mankind: Heretical Reflections on Today's Values, Culture and Politics*, [Pergamon Press, Oxford, 1978], Oneworld Publications, London.

Lutz, Mark A. and Kenneth Lux (1979) *The Challenge of Humanistic Economics*, The Benjamin/Cummings Publishing Company, Menlo Park, California.

Meadows, Donella H., Dennis L. Meadows, Jorgen Randers and William W. Behrens III (1972) *The Limits to Growth: A Report for The Club of Rome's Project on the Predicament of Mankind*, Universe Books, New York.

Meadows, Donella H., Dennis L. Meadows and Jorgen Randers (1992) *Beyond the Limits: Confronting Global Collapse, Envisioning a Sustainable Future*, Chelsea Green, Post Mills, Vermont.

Miller, John H. (1994) *Curing World Poverty: The New Role of Property*, Social Justice Review, St Louis, Missouri. [Not seen.]

Raine, Kathleen (1993) 'Global Unity and the Arts', pp. 151–7, in Suheil Bushrui, Iraj Ayman and Ervin Laszlo (eds), *Transition to a Global Society*, Oneworld Publications, Oxford.

Robertson, James (1989) *Future Wealth: A New Economics for the 21st Century*, Cassell Publishers, London and New York.

Russell, Peter (1994) 'Who's Kidding Whom? Is Western Civilization Compatible with Sustainable Development?', *World Business Academy Perspectives* 8(1): 5–21.

Schnapper, Edith B. (comp) (1952) *One in All: An Anthology of Religion from the Sacred Scriptures of the Living Faiths*, John Murray, London.

Schumacher, E.F. (1973) *Small Is Beautiful: A Study of Economics as if People Mattered*, Abacus, London.

Shoghi Effendi (1938) *The World Order of Bahá'u'lláh*, Bahá'í Publishing Trust, Wilmette, Illinois.

Tévoédjrè, Albert (1978) *La pauvreté, richesse des peuples*, Economie et Humanisme series, Les Editions Ouvrières, Paris.

UNCED (1992) *Agenda 21: The United Nations Programme of Action from Rio*, United Nations, New York.

UNDP (1995) *Human Development Report 1995* (annual editions), Oxford University Press, New York.

Universal House of Justice (1985) *The Promise of World Peace*, Bahá'í World Centre, Haifa, Israel.

Weigel, George and Robert Royal (eds) (1993) *Building the Free Society: Democracy, Capitalism and Catholic Social Teaching*, William B. Eerdman Publishing Company, Grand Rapids, Michigan, and Ethics and Public Policy Center, Washington, DC.

World Commission on Environment and Development (1987) *Our Common Future*, Oxford University Press, Oxford.

Index